The Quest for Utopia

Jewish Political Ideas and Institutions Through the Ages

The Quest for Utopia

Jewish Political Ideas and Institutions Through the Ages

Edited by **Zvi Gitelman**

M.E. Sharpe, Inc. • Armonk, New York • London, England

Library of Congress Cataloging-in-Publication Data

The Quest for Utopia: Jewish political ideas and institutions through the ages /
edited by Zvi Gitelman.
p.   cm.
Includes index.
ISBN 1-56324-061-0 (cloth).
ISBN 1-56324-062-9 (pbk.)
1. Jews—Politics and government.
2. Judaism and politics.
3. Judaism and state.
I. Gitelman, Zvi Y.
DS140.Q47   1992
323.1'1924—dc20
91-40324
CIP

Printed in the United States of America
The paper used in this publication meets the minimum
requirements of American National Standard for
Information Sciences—Permanence of Paper for
Printed Library Materials, ANSI Z 39.48-1984.

MV   10   9   8   7   6   5   4   3   2   1

CONTENTS

Acknowledgments

The ideas presented in the following chapters were first tested at a symposium at the University of Michigan sponsored by the Shanik-Fleisher Family Foundation, the Anti-Defamation League of B'nai Brith, and the Frankel Center for Judaic Studies at the university. To these institutions and to Frankel Center director Todd Edelman we owe a debt of gratitude for their support, patience, and understanding.

Introduction

ZVI GITELMAN

The emerging study of Jewish political ideas, institutions, and behavior has alerted us to the existence of a Jewish political tradition. This tradition has developed over some three thousand years and has ranged over several continents and many cultures. It has intersected with many other traditions and has evolved in conditions of Jewish sovereignty as well as in the Jewish dispersion.

Several of the contributors to this volume have pioneered in identifying and uncovering the sources of Jewish notions about the political world. They have shown that, while there may be no corpus of "classic" texts of Jewish political theory, nor does the latter add up to a systematic philosophy, there are important ideas that can be teased out of texts, generalizations that can be extrapolated from the history of Jewish communal institutions, and patterns that can be discerned in the behavior of Jews as a group.

The exploration of Jewish political traditions is of general interest because it adds to the repertoire of thought and experience on which the comparative study of politics draws. The Jewish experience is particularly rich because of its long span and its development under a multitude of conditions. Jews have developed strategies for dealing with sovereignty as well as with the lack of political autonomy. As one of the longest surviving extraterritorial peoples in the world, Jews have developed political techniques—not always successful—for survival in hostile environments. Their experience has much to teach us about ethnopolitics in multiethnic settings. Moreover, Jewish politics in the diaspora has been both externally and internally oriented. Jews have devised ways of interacting with larger communities and of organizing themselves. Since the status and aspirations of an ethnic group are defined by the group itself as well as by the state and society in which the group lives, it is important to understand the self-perceptions and communal organizations of that group as a first step toward comprehending the ways in which the group interacts with the state and the larger society.

The essays in this volume trace the development of Jewish political thinking, institutions, and behavior from biblical times to the present. In light of the long time span of Jewish history and the diversity of cultures in which it has been played out, it is not surprising that the Jewish tradition is not monolithic. But there is at least one common thread that runs through much of the tradition. That is what I have called "the quest for utopia." This is a search to improve the world, for *tikun olam*. There is no ideal polity in classical Judaism. It can accommodate monarchy as well as democracy. But there are ethical and moral standards and a striving to perfect society. As Stuart A. Cohen shows in his chapter in this volume, the Bible points to a "holy polity" in which "mankind (and especially the children of Israel) might align human action with divine inspiration." Cohen demonstrates that some basic ideas of "Western political humanism" are found in the Bible: the Bible contributes significantly to Western political discourse. Cohen's chapter identifies three seminal political ideas in the Bible and concentrates on one of them, the separation and sharing of powers. In ancient Israel, kings, priests, and prophets were independent of each other but also interdependent. All three derived their divine mandate from parallel processes of covenant and were equally authoritative mediating instruments between God and the people. Cohen compares theory and practice in ancient Israel and analyzes the power struggles among the triad of authorities. While theory seemed to prescribe a specific mode of political conduct and governmental organization, one mode of power sharing, it required a constant adjustment of the relationships within the king–priest–prophet triad to keep practice close to theory. But the very concept of power sharing has had a profound impact on the development of political thinking in the West.

The difference between a utopian vision and earthly practice is also analyzed by Gerald J. Blidstein in his discussion of ideal law and real law, comparing Muslim and Jewish concepts. Blidstein moves us from the biblical to the rabbinic period as he shows how the distinction between ideal and real law influenced rabbinic evaluations of the Israelite monarchy and of the courts. Medieval Jewish authorities were willing to accord discretionary powers and the right to employ extraordinary powers to political authorities in order to enable them to meet the real demands on those responsible for public safety and order. As Blidstein hints, this precedent has important implications for contemporary Israel as well as for the nature of authority in diaspora communities.

As noted, the Jewish political tradition encompasses politics within communities. Robert Chazan concludes from his examination of premodern communal authority that medieval Jewish communities derived support from three sources: the non-Jewish political establishment, the defensive needs of the Jewish minority, and the Judaic tradition. Chazan demonstrates how the nature of medieval governance allowed Jews considerable communal autonomy. Specifying the sanctions that each of the three supportive elements could employ, Chazan traces both the cooperation and the conflict that arose from the intersection of the three. In the face of great challenges, medieval Jews designed strategies for self-governance that were to serve them well in later periods.

In the modern period, Jews in Western and Eastern Europe created distinct political styles and traditions. Paula E. Hyman shows that West European Jews generally defined themselves as Jews by religion, not nationality, and worked for equal rights and emancipation by means of lobbying and public advocacy. Their "utopia" was, for the most part, a pluralistic, liberal, bourgeois society. East European Jews, on the other hand, thought of themselves as Jews by both religion and nationality. Their aims were more utopian than those of West European Jews. They sought either to liquidate the diaspora and create a utopian society in Palestine or to revolutionize the entire world along socialist lines. Some even sought to do both—to create both a Jewish socialist state and a socialist world.

While accepting the basic contrast between West and East European Jewry, Jonathan Frankel demonstrates that reality was more complex and he attempts to refine our understanding of it. He shows how political cultures of different countries, including the United States, influenced Jewish political thinking and action. East European Jewish politics was marked by radical ebbs and flows. Many movements were compelled to modify utopian policies in the face of changing realities. Frankel sees a triangle of forces in modern Jewish political behavior: traditionalist, emancipationist, and auto-emancipationist. Despite their differences, these often interacted and overlapped. Frankel, like the other authors, points to elements in contemporary Israeli and American Jewish politics that derive from European precedents.

Both West and East European traditions shaped American Jewish politics. But, as Peter Y. Medding shows, American Jewry has developed a distinct political style, especially since World War II. Jews now demand a share of power and have integrated their agenda into the mainstream of American politics. Lobbies have replaced the *shtadlanim* (intercessors), concern has shifted from defense of rights to other issues, and Jews have drifted away somewhat from their traditional political liberalism. In recent years, local Jewish federations have become political actors. Jews have become professional politicians and "insiders." Larger numbers of upper-middle-class Jews are now involved in politics. There has been a substantial increase in the number of candidates for office who are Jews, many of them from outside the major centers of Jewish population. New lobbying groups have emerged. The Orthodox community has been activated politically. There are "new threats, new allies, and split coalitions" that make American Jewish political life dynamic and complex.

Jewish conceptions of covenant and the sharing of powers imply limitations on the use of power even in the noblest quest for the best possible society. Although they have suffered at the hands of groups convinced that they were organizing the best of all possible worlds, Jews retain their confidence in the perfectability of the world and of mankind. However, they go about the quest for utopia with a strong awareness of their own and of mankind's limitations. The search for a better world must be a reasoned, realistic one. The essays in this book describe and analyze the way Jews have conducted that search over the centuries.

Contributors

Gerald J. Blidstein holds the Miriam Martha Hubert Chair in Jewish Law at the Ben-Gurion University of the Negev.

Robert Chazan is professor of Hebraic and Jewish studies at New York University.

Stuart A. Cohen is professor of political studies at Bar-Ilan University in Ramat-Gan.

Jonathan Frankel is professor of Russian studies at the Hebrew University of Jerusalem and an editor of *Studies in Contemporary Judaism*.

Zvi Gitelman is professor of political science and Tisch Professor of Judaic Studies at the University of Michigan, Ann Arbor.

Paula E. Hyman is Lucy Moses Professor of Modern Jewish History at Yale University.

Peter Y. Medding is professor of political science at the Hebrew University of Jerusalem and an editor of *Studies in Contemporary Judaism*.

The
Quest
for
Utopia

Jewish
Political
Ideas
and
Institutions
Through
the Ages

Comparative Politics and the Jewish Political Experience

ZVI GITELMAN

The study of Jewish political ideas, institutions, and behavior could enrich the field of comparative politics and at the same time deepen our understanding of the history and nature of Judaism and the Jewish people. Such analysis has only begun, but its first fruits hold out the promise of a useful, intellectually rewarding enterprise. It is thus surprising that none of the major texts in comparative politics, or for that matter any of the outstanding monographs in the field, devotes attention to the Jewish political tradition. This chapter attempts to suggest in schematic form some ways in which our understanding of political phenomena and of the Jewish people and their history might be enhanced by confronting the field of comparative politics with that tradition.

The enterprise of comparative politics is an attempt to understand political phenomena, such as institutions, processes, and behavior, by gathering empirical information on political systems and trying to extract from it the essence of how these phenomena work. The ultimate aim is to identify the regularities in the workings of the political world—what the Russians call *zakonomernosti*. Most political scientists see this aim as a heuristic device rather than a realizable goal. Nevertheless, the greater the number of "real world" cases included in the evidentiary base, the more powerful the generalizations at which one can arrive. The case studies forming that evidentiary base can be either contemporary, as most are, or historical.

Comparative politics therefore tries to achieve comprehensiveness, realism, and precision.[1] However, since political life is not conducted in controlled laboratory conditions, comparative politics falls short in respect to all three goals. Our study of political systems is constrained by our limited access to information about contemporary systems, let alone those systems that existed in the past. It is further impeded by subjectivity and the intrusion of preconceptions, prejudices, and personal preferences. The normative and the empirical are probably more difficult to separate in political analysis than they are in, say, biological or chemical analysis. Political studies are further limited by the variability and unpredictability of human behavior. These make it infinitely more difficult to measure, much less predict, political behavior than to measure and predict mathematical, physical, or even biological phenomena. Therefore, any body of evidence that can be added to the store of our knowledge of politics is to be welcomed. That alone should be sufficient motivation for studying the Jewish political experience and adding our findings to the corpus of political science. As Apter and Eckstein note, "the task of science is the reasoned interpretation of experience through the discovery of valid generalizations and the application of such generalizations to specific events. Science seeks theoretical and useful knowledge, to which both the unique and the familiar may contribute."[2]

A more parochial reason for studying Jewish political ideas and experiences is for Jews to understand themselves better. While some insist on viewing Judaism as independent of historical and societal context, most scholars would, on the contrary, stress its evolution in interaction with a wide variety of environments. Jewish culture—that is, Jewish perceptions and patterned ways of doing things—has developed in confrontation, sometimes conflictual, sometimes cooperative, with other cultures. Judaism and Jewish culture have retained their distinctive characteristics, and have infused some of them into other religions and cultures, but they have been influenced and shaped by them in turn. When we apply the concepts, insights, and techniques of comparative politics, we are better able to appreciate why Jews think about the political world as they do and why they behave in it as they do. As Dogan and Pelassy observe, "We gain knowledge through reference.... We compare to evaluate more objectively our situation as individuals, a community, or a nation."[3]

A third compelling reason for examining Jewish political thought, institutions, and behavior is that these have been unusual and even unique in significant ways. Most striking is the longevity, adaptability, and capacity for survival of a people and a faith that began in the ancient Near East and alone among the civilizations of that era has survived in recognizable form until this day. This occurred despite the fact that the Hebrews (Jews) were far from the most powerful people of ancient times and for most of their history have been inferior in numbers and power to their neighbors and to peoples among whom they resided as a minority. Is there a "formula" that explains this survival? Could it be transferred and adapted to other peoples; and, if not, what special circumstances explain this historical aberrant?

Before embarking on a study of the Jewish political experience one must define its parameters. For purposes of this discussion, I would set those parameters as widely as possible, encompassing periods of Jewish political sovereignty as well as periods when Jews lacked political autonomy. The time can extend from biblical times to the present, and the geographical compass could include the political experiences of Jews wherever they have lived in the course of the centuries. This does not mean to imply that there have not been sharp breaks in Jewish history or that there is a constant of uniquely Jewish characteristics that makes its mark on all experience and at all times. It merely suggests that there may be valuable lessons to be learned, both by political scientists and by those interested in Jewish history and culture, from the great variety of experiences in which Jews have been involved.

There is one rough way in which those experiences can be usefully divided. It probably makes sense to examine the Jewish political experience separately for those periods when the Jews enjoyed political sovereignty, or even autonomy, and those when they did not. The political tasks, assets, and liabilities of a people are quite different under these two sets of circumstances and call for a differentiated treatment. The situation in which sovereignty is enjoyed ought to be refined further, perhaps, into the first period of sovereignty and the contemporary one.

The First Period of Sovereignty

One might set the boundaries of this era by beginning with the formation of the Jewish people, continuing through the attainment of national self-consciousness and statehood, and ending with the definitive loss of independence and the exile in the year 70. The biblical account of the emergence of the Jewish (Hebrew) people is almost an anthropological textbook account of social evolution. One man, Abraham, begins both a religion and a people. A nuclear family committed to that faith evolves into an extended family that becomes a clan. A national identity begins to emerge when the Israelites constitute a distinct group, inhabiting a particular territory (Goshen), and set apart by their religious, economic, and perhaps linguistic characteristics, in a foreign land, Egypt. This minority is discriminated against, is unable to achieve accommodation with the host society, and leaves it.

In the transition from being a minority without sovereignty to achieving a territory of their own, these people acquire a highly specified set of religious rules interwoven with a less specified and more flexible set of principles that are to guide their social and political organization. There is little differentiation between cultic rules and those governing economics, social organization, and political structure and behavior, except that there seems to be less specification of the latter. Thus, the Israelites are not given a prescribed form of government, nor are they proscribed from particular forms, in contrast to the rather specific regulations that govern their dietary, ritual, and economic practices. The Book of Deuteronomy does, however, provide for a future political evolution when it describes circumstances under which a monarchy might emerge and specifies limitations on that monarchy. In the Book of Samuel the prescriptions and proscriptions mentioned in Deuteronomy receive their practical application when the Israelites demand of the Prophet Samuel a king so that they might be "like the other nations." The emergence of the monarchy is a clear example of a tendency that is to characterize the Jewish people throughout the centuries: a desire to conform to what they perceive as the universal practice, the tendency toward assimilation. The biblical account, both in Deuteronomy and in Samuel, makes it quite clear that the monarchy is a concession by God to human nature's desire for conformity and need for a concrete, earthly leadership rather than strict reliance on guidance by an abstract god, albeit one who speaks through the mouths of his designated representatives.

The evolution of leadership in biblical Israel is itself worthy of analysis. From the leadership provided by the head of a clan it shifts to leadership attained by a person selected by God (Moses). But that leader is intensely human. Although he enjoys familiarity with the culture of the power elite of Egypt, he is handicapped in his role as articulator of the interests of the Israelites and must rely on a spokesman. He is a poor administrator, and must rely on the scheme proposed by his father-in-law, a priest of another religion, for the establishment of a judicial and administrative system that will make efficient governance possible. Authority begins to be decentralized, as judges and tribal chieftains legitimately assume governmental functions. Leadership is no longer passed from father to son, but through a mysterious process of selection by God. The mystery and unpredictability of the process are emphasized in the resolution of the challenge posed to Moses by Korach and his group. Korach's arguments are prima facie so powerful that Moses is incapable of defeating them on rational-legal grounds. Moses "falls on his face" and begs for divine guidance in meeting Korach's challenge. Korach is defeated, not by logical argument or by reference to constitutional provisions, but by a violent assertion by God of his right to choose a leader without fully explaining his choice.

For several generations after Moses's designated successor, Joshua, leaders seem to emerge in response to military challenges. If a woman, Deborah, is more capable of leading Israel in battle than her male peers, so be it. After proving her military abilities, she seems to be entitled to exercise civil authority and leadership. Even a person of dubious lineage, the son of a harlot (Yiftakh), becomes a leader by virtue of his military prowess. Leadership, then, is gained by achievement and not by ascription.

However, there is a countervailing leadership, that of the priests, that is gained by ascription, though it can be lost by malfeasance (Nadav and Avihu). The priests have their own areas of responsibility and the other kinds of leaders largely respect the distinction. Later, the division of power seems to be more between monarchs and prophets, the latter serving as the conscience of the king and as his guide (Samuel and Saul, Nathan and David). They can do so because the king is under what might fairly be called constitutional restraints.

The Book of Deuteronomy specifies limitations on the power of a king, including upper limits on his wealth, the number of wives he may take, and the number of horses he may keep. Maimonides calculates that the king has twenty-three commandments or obligations given explicitly to him.[4] Perhaps the most interesting, from the viewpoint of politics, is the obligation on the king to write a Torah scroll. Has a king nothing better to do than assume the role of a scribe and spend many months inscribing a Torah scroll? The reason seems to be that this is a most immediate and constant reminder to the king that there is a law above him, that his authority exists only within the bounds of that higher law, and that he is not exempt from the obligations that devolve on his subjects. Maimonides comments that the king must possess two scrolls, one of which remains in his library, and the other of which travels with him everywhere—on the battlefield, in court, at meal times.[5] The point is made again when it is stated that someone who violates the commandment of a king because he is engaged in fulfilling another divine commandment, even a minor one, is not considered to have done wrong, because "the word of the teacher takes precedence over the word of the slave."[6] Thus, we seem to have a kind of constitutional monarchy here, with the Torah serving as the constitution. This is but one aspect of the broader concept of mutual obligations that exist between men and God and among men and which are elaborated upon in the Bible and in Rabbinic literature. Daniel Elazar calls this the "covenant idea." He describes it as a "morally grounded perpetual . . . compact between parties having independent but not necessarily equal status, which established certain mutual obligations and a commitment to undertake joint action to achieve defined ends which may be limited or comprehensive, under conditions of mutual respect and in such a way as to protect the fundamental integrity of all parties involved."[7] This very early expression of concepts later denominated as "social contract theory" needs to be examined for its notions of civic and other kinds of obligation, of authority and its limits, and of the relationship between elites and non-elites. It is worth remembering that biblical ideas shaped the thinking of Locke, Hobbes, Rousseau, and others, who were much more familiar with these biblical texts than are most of our contemporaries.

In addition to concepts of leadership and constitutionalism, the Bible also addresses the issue of how a people should organize itself internally. There is a modest amount of material presented about the administrative structure of the Israelites, first in the wilderness, and later in the Land of Canaan. It seems, however, that not until the reign of King Solomon, when the functionaries of the palace and the provincial administrators are described, was a formal system of public administration instituted.

A fourth political issue that arises most prominently in the first period of Jewish sovereignty is the relationship between moral/religious and civil/military authorities. Moses and Joshua are perhaps the last leaders to incorporate fully both political and religious leadership.

These functions seem to become more and more differentiated over time until the triad of priest, prophet, and king emerges. Like all separations of power, this one is not without its conflicts and tensions: Who should decide moral issues? Who provides moral guidance to the people? To what extent are rulers subordinate to religious leaders, and vice versa? Should religious or civic needs take precedence? Daniel Elazar suggests that "the Jewish political tradition is federal . . . in orientation. Fundamentally, federalism involves the coming together of separate elements to compound a common entity in such a way that their respective integrities are preserved. . . . There has hardly been an age when the Jewish *edah* [community] has not been organized on a federal basis."[8] This introduces an important variant on the theme of shared powers. Powers may be shared not only among civil and religious authorities but also in federal arrangements among civil authorities themselves.

The Jewish Political Experience in the Diaspora

The long experience of the Jewish people in the diaspora, deprived of sovereignty and a territory of their own, raises quite a different set of issues from the ones dealt with before. Especially since there are not many parallel historical cases, people have sought an explanation for the survival of the Jews as a distinct entity despite their being widely dispersed and persecuted or, on the other hand, given ample opportunity to assimilate. Some have found theological explanations, others sociological ones, but it seems that few have looked to political analysis for an explanation of the phenomenon. Could it be that the internal organization of Jews—admittedly almost always around a commitment to a portable faith which, while it has a territorial focus, can exist outside the territory—is part of the explanation of their capacity to survive? What is there about that organization that proved to be effective? This opens up an entire field of inquiry that has not been ploughed: How do ethnic groups deal with the loss of sovereignty?

Perhaps one of the first things such groups do is develop a theory to explain what happened to them. Both the Jews and the Poles, for example, have done so in theological terms. The Jewish literature is full of references to the exile as a punishment for Israel's sins. After the Poles lost their state to their neighbor empires in the eighteenth century, Romantic writers such as Mickiewicz, Slowacki, and Krasinski presented the image of Poland as the "Christ among nations," the Catholic nation destined to suffer for the sins of others but then to be resurrected to bring salvation to all the nations. With the reconstitution of Jewish and Polish states came controversy over their boundaries and, especially in the Jewish case, disagreement over the theological significance of the reconstitution of a sovereign state.

Jews, Poles, Czechs, Slovaks, Armenians, and a host of others developed strategies for their survival as ethnic groups after having lost political independence. It would be instructive to discover which strategies succeeded more than others, and why. The Jewish case would have to figure prominently in any such analysis.

A second area for comparative research is the question of how ethnic groups establish or re-establish sovereignty. In the post–World War II era we are especially impressed by the number of peoples that have gone from colonial to sovereign rule, but we should remember that many peoples have failed in this attempt even in our own time. Analysis of the development of the Zionist movement and the establishment of the state of Israel should be of as much interest to students of comparative politics as the revival of Hebrew is to sociolinguists.

The Jewish political experience in the diaspora should also be instructive in another way. For at least the past century, Jews have been politically active in Europe and North America, not only as individuals, but also as consciously Jewish groups (parties, lobbying organizations). There has been an interesting evolution in the political power of American Jews in the last half-century. Because of increasing levels of education and wealth among American Jews, they have been better positioned to exercise political influence than they were before, or than are some other American ethnic groups at present. But what is more interesting, perhaps, than the change in Jewish political power in America is the evolution of Jewish attitudes toward that power. In the 1930s there was considerable hesitancy in mobilizing Jewish political influence and a great deal of discomfort in "showing it" publicly or even privately. Scholars are still debating what consequences this may have had for European Jewry after the rise of Hitler. Since World War II, and perhaps especially since the Six-Day War in the Middle East, American Jews have become more conscious of their political power, and also more willing to deploy it. It would be useful to analyze the changes both in political influence and in attitudes toward its use and to compare these with the behavior of other ethnic groups in the United

States (or elsewhere). We might be able to arrive at a more sophisticated understanding of "ethnic politics."

Finally, there has been a good deal of research on the internal political life of diaspora Jewish communities, but surely more could be
done. This relates directly to the question of how ethnic groups perceive, acquire, and use political power. One of the components of such
power must be the internal organization of the group and its own
political styles. Such investigation would no doubt be enriched by
reference to organization theory, including studies of organizations that
have outlived their "transitive" functions (achieving goals beyond the
enhancement of the organization itself) but persist through dedication
to their "reflexive" functions.[9]

In sum, the Jewish political experience in different lands is a rich
data base for the study of various questions dealt with by comparative
politics and could, in turn, be illuminated by the application of the
concepts of comparative politics.[10]

The Second Period of Sovereignty

When considering the state of Israel as a political phenomenon, one
may legitimately ask to what extent it grows organically out of the
Jewish political tradition. Obviously, were it not for Jewish continuity,
no one would have bothered to attempt the revival of a Jewish state.
Yet, when that state was established in 1948 it did not draw from the
Jewish classical sources or from the Jewish diaspora experience for its
structures. The founders could not even agree on a constitution to set
down the defining principles and character of the state. Instead, the
party and administrative systems drew largely from the precedents of
Eastern Europe (Poland, especially; not Russia, as is commonly believed), from which most of the founders had come, and of England,
whose mandate over Palestine left its stamp on the political life of the
country. There was no return to the Israelite monarchy, because the
consensus was that a "modern democracy" was the most desirable
mode of political organization.

The Jewish character of the state of Israel remains undefined. This
is manifested in a variety of issues, such as the debate over amending
the Law of Return, which are among the most contentious in a polity
that has no lack of thorny issues. The fact that there is so much interest
in such matters attests to the commitment of Israeli Jews, however

expressed, to taking seriously the Jewish character of the state. But neither Israelis nor diaspora Jews have yet figured out how to fuse Jewish political traditions with the modern democratic ones to which almost all are committed. Those who reject the fusion and opt for only one of these elements—the late Meir Kahane would be one example and some extreme leftists might be another—find themselves on the edges of the political spectrum. Thus, Israel poses an interesting analytic case, relevant to other societies (India, Saudi Arabia, Egypt, Iran, Turkey) that are challenged to combine traditional and modern political modes. Some political sociologists—the Israeli S.N. Eisenstadt comes to mind—have studied the question of combining modernity and tradition in emergent states, but perhaps Israel has not been studied enough from this perspective, probably because it was assumed (erroneously, in my opinion) that Israel was already a "modern" society and would become even more so with the passage of time. In fact, it would appear that in Israel a modern superstructure sits atop a society that is only partly modernized and is not necessarily becoming more secular, technologically oriented, or pluralistic.

Israel is also an excellent example of several political phenomena much discussed in the literature on comparative politics. For the purposes of our discussion, they need only be listed:

(1) *National integration.* How does one build a stable state out of people coming from many and highly diverse political cultures?

(2) *Political and military survival.* Not a few states face the kind of international isolation, military threats, and economic threats that Israel does, but not many face all three, and to such an acute degree. On the other hand, few have such a powerful and supportive ally as Israel does in the United States. How Israel has dealt with multiple challenges and constant crisis is not only intellectually interesting but of great practical importance.

(3) *Cultural revival.* While not a strict political matter, this question—which includes linguistic and literary revival, renewal of scholarship and folklore and so on—is one where the state is involved to a great extent. Whereas the Irish have failed to revive Gaelic, Israel has succeeded with Hebrew. Whereas other states have managed to accommodate different ethnic sub-cultures, Israel has tended, like America, to homogenize them. The role of the state in the revival, suppression, and management of culture is one that lends itself to comparative study.

(4) *Integration of ethnic/religious minorities.* One of the ironies of Israel is that a state dominated by a people who have perhaps the longest experience in the world as an ethnic minority has not yet devised a satisfactory way of dealing with its own ethnic and religious minorities. Israel must be factored into any comparative analysis of state-building and the management of ethnic integration.

(5) *Political institutions.* Israel has been discussed in the literature on proportional representation and coalition building.[11] It has been used to demonstrate the limitations of the theory of minimum winning coalitions and to test other theories of how coalitions are constructed. The idea of a "dominant party system" was expanded on the basis of the experience of Israel and Italy, one which has been shared by India, Japan, interwar Czechoslovakia, the Federal Republic of Germany, and other countries. In teaching American students the intricacies of multi-party systems, the subtleties of proportional representation, and the mysteries of coalition building, I have found Israel to be a manageable, intriguing, and accessible case study.

(6) *Electoral behavior.* There are good data from electoral surveys going back to 1969, covering five Israeli national elections. Asher Arian has organized and reported many of these surveys, which have been designed with American and European models in mind. This means that cross-national comparison with Israeli data is quite easy. Israeli electoral history has been very interesting, and many of the dominant variables in electoral studies—religion, ethnicity, class, education—are salient in Israeli society. Israel can be used effectively to demonstrate the impact of these variables, and many others, on political behavior.

(7) *The military and the state.* This is a subject that has been analyzed in Western democracies, Communist states, and the Third World. The Israeli case is especially interesting because Israel does not fall clearly within any of those categories and, even more so, because in few countries is the military as important. Some work has been done on the Israeli case[12] and it has caught the attention of some of those doing comparative analyses.

(8) *Strategies of economic development.* Many countries that gained independence after 1945 have debated vigorously what kind of economic system to adopt. Israel's economic development has some unique features—labor-owned (Histadrut) enterprises, communal farms (*kibbutzim*), massive infusions of private and governmental for-

eign aid—that should add some interesting dimensions to those debates. Studying the Israeli experience could certainly benefit other emerging countries, especially those poor in natural resources.

(9) *Political/cultural isolation.* Israel is the least "typical" Middle Eastern state, and course titles in some universities reflect this ("Politics of the Arab Middle East"). Its political structures derive from Europe and do not resemble those of the other countries in the region; it has a large population of European origin; it is a democracy; its language and religion are unique. How does such a political misfit survive? This is not a problem unique to Israel. Czechoslovakia was the only democratic country in interwar East Central Europe; the USSR was the only Communist country in the world until the late 1940s; Venezuela has been a democracy when most of its neighbors were not; South Africa is economically and culturally different and politically isolated from its neighbors. Such situations raise domestic issues (such as "capitalist encirclement" for the USSR and "Levantization" for Israel). The domestic and foreign policy implications of such situations have not been sufficiently explored, nor has understanding of Israel's position been enhanced by reference to these other cases.

Conclusion

The Jewish political experience is a rich storehouse of information and ideas that have hardly been touched by the literature in comparative politics. Those who find comparative politics a useful enterprise will want to investigate the Jewish experience both for its unique features and for those it shares with the political experiences of other peoples. Those who are interested in understanding the evolution and staying power of the Jewish people might benefit from the insights of comparative politics and from research on the historical experiences of other peoples. The state of Israel presents a challenge to those who seek to distill the defining characteristics of the Jewish political tradition. Comparative analysis may clarify some of the issues that have agitated Israel and put them into perspective. This exercise could take the edge off some arguments about the "Jewish character" of the state, though these are so laden with emotion and so entangled in political and personal interests that one cannot be very sanguine that academic analysis would change the tone, let alone the substance, of the discussion. For students of comparative politics, as for other social scientists, Israel is an excellent laboratory in which many central issues can be studied. In short, the application of the approaches of comparative politics to the Jewish political experience, from ancient times to the present, could enrich our understanding of both politics and of Jewish experiences.

Notes

1. Gabriel Almond and G. Bingham Powell, *Comparative Politics: A Developmental Approach* (Boston: Little, Brown, 1966), p. 9.
2. David Apter and Harry Eckstein, *Comparative Politics* (New York: The Free Press, 1963), p. v.
3. Mattei Dogan and Dominique Pelassy, *How to Compare Nations* (Chatham, NJ: Chatham House, 1984), p. 3.
4. *Mishneh Torah*, Hilkhot Melachim, I,1.
5. Ibid.
6. Ibid., I,9.
7. Daniel J. Elazar, ed., *Kinship and Consent: The Jewish Political Tradition and Its Contemporary Uses* (Washington, DC: University Press of America, 1983), p. 9.
8. Ibid., p. 5.
9. See, for example, Lawrence B. Mohr, "The Concept of Organizational Goal," *American Political Science Review*, 16, no. 4 (December 1971).
10. It should be noted that because of my ignorance of the Jewish experience in non-European settings I have probably missed a great number of fascinating and important issues that might otherwise have been included in these observations, drawn almost exclusively from European and North American cases.
11. See, for example, Gregory Mahler and Richard Trilling, "Coalition Behavior and Cabinet Formation: The Case of Israel," *Comparative Political Studies*, 9, no. 2 (July 1975).
12. See, for example, Yoram Peri, *Between Battles and Ballots* (New York: Cambridge University Press, 1983).

Kings, Priests, and Prophets

Patterns of Constitutional Discourse and Constitutional Conflict in Ancient Israel

STUART A. COHEN

The foundation of the Jewish political tradition is to be found in the Bible and its rabbinic interpretation. Unlike products of the classical and Western traditions of political philosophy, the Old Testament offers no precisely reasoned statement of constitutional principles. Neither does it set forth formally architectured statements of political theory. In this matter, as in others, the Bible's style is characteristically elliptical and discursive. Its account of ancient Israel's experiments with various political systems and regimes is invariably descriptive; only fleetingly are the separate portraits of specific incidents accompanied by an explicit evaluation of their respective constitutional implications. Interpretations of their merits and failings have to be deduced from comparative analyses of the narrative and judicial portions of the text. As Daniel Elazar has pointed out, "Biblical political teachings must be discovered in the same manner that other Biblical knowledge must emerge, by careful examination and analysis of the text, with careful attention to recurring patterns and the reconciliation of apparent contradictions."[1]

This chapter is intended as a contribution to that inquiry. Without denying the rich texture of individual political achievements—and fiascoes—recounted in the scriptural chronicles, it will attempt to show that the cumulative impact of those narratives is the articulation of a distinct set of constitutional doctrines, several of which have been assimilated as integral components of all Western political thought. Collectively, the teachings enunciated in the Old Testament provide an inspiration for political practice and a prescription for the foundation and maintenance of the perfect political order. As such, they complement the moral principles enshrined in the text, placing them in a communal and institutional setting. The holy polity, they teach, is the medium whereby mankind (and especially the children of Israel) might align human action with divine inspiration.

To assert the existence of a distinctively biblical perspective on political power and its exercise is not to claim that the Old Testament necessarily invented each of its own political notions. Still less, of course, is it to identify that text as the only influence on the subsequent reformulation of those concepts and their enrichment in the seminal works of Western political theory. This chapter does not, therefore, claim a biblical monopoly for the principle of constitutionalism in antiquity. Neither does it posit an exclusively biblical parentage for the liberal tradition of political practice in modern times. What it attempts to show, however, is the distinctive style and language in which some of the notions considered most fundamental in Western political humanism are incorporated in the Old Testament and the particular rigor with which their implications are explored there. For all its untidy complexity, Judaism's earliest literature does impart a sustained political message, whose scope is throughout coherent with the sublime character of all of its societal and individual teachings. In that fusion lies the particular contribution of ancient Israel's experience and culture to the later development of all political discourse. Of the Bible's several specific constitutional teachings, two have been most assiduously studied in the secondary literature. Respectively termed the concepts of theocratic government and covenantal partnership, they are also conventionally regarded as the areas in which the Old Testament's contribution to subsequent political thought has proved to have been most enduring. In its later renditions, the theocratic notion implies that the ends of political activity are intrinsically moral in nature. Indeed, political concerns possess spiritual dimensions which transcend their immediately material thrust. Good governments reflect and articulate that ethos; the best governments—which, by definition, are governments by God—also stimulate it. Consequently (and this is the second of the Bible's primary messages), the legitimacy of individual regimes is ultimately contingent upon the degree to which they are both true to the values of the polity and commensurate with the ethical interests of its various components. Covenants, involving God as well as humans, are the consensual means whereby—in biblical terms—the separate rights of both are confirmed and preserved.

While acknowledging the pivotal importance and influence of those two concepts, I suggest that biblical Judaism also contributed a third teaching to the traditions that have become part of the Western constitutional heritage. From the biblical perspective political perfection is not solely the product of direct divine governance. Neither is its attainment entirely dependent upon the inspiration granted to charismatic individuals. Much though the Old Testament emphasizes the necessity for personal righteousness (especially by public figures), it also suggests a structural framework within which the political authority delegated to such persons might be constitutionalized and thereby legitimated. In the last analysis, it posits, political virtue is embodied in a governmental system that—under God—formally distributes human rulership amongst specifically accredited jurisdictional domains. A separation and sharing of powers thus institutionalizes the qualities that the concepts of theocracy and covenant have themselves inspired.

The biblical ideal of power-sharing is not severely compartmentalized from either of the text's other two great constitutional themes. Rather, it is portrayed as a necessary complement to theocratic and covenantal government, interacting with those concepts and reinforcing their mutual resonance. Nevertheless, for the purposes of analysis this chapter will discuss the three separately, placing particular (and admittedly disproportionate) emphasis on the Bible's analysis of the theory and practice of power-sharing. What the Old Testament offers is a protracted commentary on a system of rule that distributes political power among three distinct clusters of human authority, personified in the public officials designated kings, priests, and prophets. At the descriptive level, this unique tripartite structure provided a tool for the understanding of ancient Israel's earliest political discourse. As a prescription for later generations, it also constructed a normative framework within which other biblical notions could find constitutional expression and instrumental articulation.

Theocracy

In its biblical meaning, the theocratic principle implies that Hebrew government is, in every sense of the term, government by God. Even at its most basic, there is far more to this teaching than the notion that the Creator of the world—by virtue of his omnipotence—possesses an unquestionable right to exercise proprietary rights over what is indubitably His domain.[2] As the Decalogue's very first commandment makes explicit, God is considered to be actively and continuously involved in the direct governance of His people; indeed, having taken the Children of Israel out of Egypt, he deserves recognition as an intrinsic segment of that government. Thereafter, He persistently takes upon himself and fulfills the roles of law-giver, judge, administrator, warrior, and—ultimately—redeemer.

Early rabbinic literature encapsulated the idea of the theocracy in the term *malkhut shamayim* (the kingdom of heaven), a phrase that—although not explicitly found in the Old Testament—aptly conveys the biblical notion that the appropriate yardstick for the measurement of all human endeavors (public and private) is God's purpose, not man's desires.[3] From this it follows that neither the polity nor its human institutions are regarded as ends in themselves. They exist solely as means to a divine end. That, essentially, is why biblical political thought does not attribute an independent right to the existence of any particular governmental framework. Although the texts do know of the *ir* (city) and *medinah* (state), scripture deliberately refrains from attributing to such entities the kind of reified status which they were later to attain in some branches of classical and Western political thought. Altogether, indeed, the Bible views political institutions—whatever their form—as little more than instruments, useful only for fostering and maintaining the good society and for facilitating the human attainment of the highest possible moral goals. It certainly denies the human rulers of such entities—even if they do appropriate God's own title of *melekh* (king)—anything other than mortal status.

One consequence of this position is that, from the moment of their accession, those rulers too are subject to God's own laws and judged by the standards of His will. A second is that, in the last analysis, Israel's human kingship is devoid of the sacral connotations attributed to governing agencies in the gentile world of the ancient Middle East.[4] Gideon's refusal to arrogate to himself a position of hereditary rulership (Judges 8:22–23), together with Samuel's initial resistance to the popular demand for the establishment of a monarchy (I Sam. 8:11–19), thus articulate what might be described as the classic biblical viewpoint. Later developments, which negated both of these positions, constitute regrettable—albeit sanctioned—regressions from the scriptural ideal.[5]

Covenant

All this is not to imply that the biblical theocracy is equivalent to a blatant divine dictatorship. Conceptions of that nature are explicitly denied by the second of scripture's great political themes, the idea of the covenant. Baldly summarized, what this notion implies is that relationships between God and mankind, and especially between God and Israel, are founded on their having come together in a unique partnership.[6] Although necessarily a compact of unequal entities, the covenant thus concluded nevertheless preserves the respective integrities of the partners and provides a basis for their co-operation in order to attain mutually agreed ends. Such was the covenant between God and mankind—as represented by Noah—after the flood (Genesis 9:8–17); such was the covenant between God and Abraham (then Abram; Genesis, chap. 18); and such—most relevant of all—was the covenant between God and the entire house of Israel at Sinai (Exodus, chaps. 19 and 20). In each case, according to the biblical account, God limited Himself drastically by recognizing the freedom of humans to contract obligations with Him and to maintain their own integrity while doing so, not simply to obey Him but to hearken to His words as covenantal partners.

Of the several political implications of this crucial concept, perhaps the most significant is that which is most straightforward. Through the process of covenant, God recognizes humans to be His partners in the perfection of His own creation. This is a breathtakingly radical notion, whose clear thrust is the declaration that all sovereignty—whatever its expression—must normatively be based upon the principle of reciprocity between rulers and ruled. Even when initiating (perhaps even imposing) His covenants with Israel, God acknowledges as much; indeed, He transcends His own covenantal stipulations when undertaking to implement them with *hesed* (covenant love; i.e. the love relationship between parties whose actions express their mutual feelings and are not merely prescribed by the terms of their contract).[7] Human sovereigns, whose scope for unilateral action is in any case more confined, must necessarily follow that example.

This theme resonates throughout the string of post-Sinaitic covenantal reaffirmations recounted in the Old Testament, and especially those concluded under the human aegis of Joshua, David, Josiah, and Ezra. Notwithstanding the differences among these individual ceremonies, all shared a striking fidelity to the Sinaitic tradition from which they derived their common inspiration. Each reiterates the consensual foundation of Israelite political association; similarly, each stresses that the partnerships thus created (and to which God is Himself witness, guarantor, and sometimes partner) are based upon an agreed recognition of the mutually binding force of the covenant-as-constitution. Indeed, it is through the covenant, as periodically mediated, that the contracting parties attain the legitimacy that entitles them to take political action. Moreover, it is from the covenant—sometimed rendered *torah*[8]—that each derives its mandate for such action.

As the early rabbis clearly understood, the biblical idea of covenantal government necessarily invoked that of responsible government. Just as the polity is not the exclusive preserve of God, neither can it be the private benefice of any single man or ruling elite. On the contrary, that order is—in the classical sense—a *res publica*, owned in common by all the ongoing partners to the original covenant by which it was first brought into being.[9] All share equally in the responsibility for creating the *malkhut shamayim,* which is the purpose of political action; all therefore possess a sanctified right (enshrined in the *torah*) to participate in the process whereby political policies are formulated and executed.

The Separation of Powers

It is tempting to extend the representative thrust of the Bible's covenant conception, and to hypothesize its translation into an avowedly democratic structure of government. Some individual passages might initially seem to justify that exercise;[10] but since most of the available texts have little to say on Israelite government at its grass roots, postulations of a general nature are necessarily speculative. Invariably, the Bible restricts its horizons to the apex of the governmental pyramid, portraying relationships within and among the ruling elite rather than between the governors and the masses of the governed.

At that hierarchical level of analysis, however, the evidence—although less populist in tone—is perhaps even more striking in implication. What emerges from the texts as a logical corollary of the covenantal principle is not democracy throughout the political system but a distinct notion of power-sharing at its highest levels. The Old Testament expresses no sympathy whatsoever for a system of government in which a single body or group possesses a monopoly of the prerogatives and privileges of political authority. Instead, it mandates that those attributes be distributed among specifically accredited domains of government. Constitutional omnipotence is occasionally and implicitly refused even to God;[11] it is permanently and explicitly denied to man.

Significantly, not even Moses—undoubtedly the most extraordinary protagonist in all Jewish history, and especially in Jewish political history—is exempted from this axiom. Accordingly, and despite his occasional incursions into the ritual domain, it was not he but his brother Aaron who was divinely designated to be High Priest. Similarly, and notwithstanding Moses's apparent invocation of various monarchical symbols, not his descendants but those of Judah were later to be invested with the title of kings.[12] Lesser mortals, whose contact with God was manifestly less intimate, had to abide by restrictions that were both more formal and more precise. Specifically, they were bound by a constitutional philosophy that mandated the diffusion of political power among the priesthood, the monarchy, and the domain of prophecy. It is to an examination of that tripartite structure, and its implications, that more detailed attention must now be turned.

If we are to follow the traditional Jewish canonical sequence, our earliest biblical evidence for a governmental triad consisting of kings, priests, and prophets is located in the sketch of governmental procedures outlined in Deuteronomy chapters 17 and 18. There, after a general prologue (17:8–13), separate paragraphs are allotted to the rights and duties of each of the public officials designated the *melekh* (king; 17:14–20), the *kohanim* and *levi'im* (priests and levites; 18:1–8), and the *navi* (prophet; 18:9–22). Parallel passages of a narrative form indicate that the structure of this arrangement was not dictated merely by administrative convenience. Rather, it reflected a conception of government that was deliberately designed to constitutionalize power-sharing in a manner that would facilitate the attainment of the theo-political ends enunciated at Sinai. Particularly significant, in this regard, is the biblical account of the historical circumstances that initially called each of these three offices into being. In all cases, the title-holders derived their authority from a separate covenant with God: the revelation to Moses established the covenant of prophecy (Exodus 34:10; Deut. 18:8 and 34:10); that with Pinhas (Aaron's grandson) gave permanent expression to the priesthood (Numb. 25:13); the covenant with the house of David bestowed everlasting institutional form on the monarchy (II Sam. 7:4–17 and Psalms 89).[13]

There is clearly more to these related accounts than an attempt at historical veracity. Implicit in the biblical reconstruction of the inauguration of the three franchises is the notion that the circumstances of their creation endowed the human embodiments of these domains, together with their legitimate lineal successors, with independent and divinely mandated authority within their respective spheres of jurisdiction. Some seven hundred years after the close of the biblical chronicle, *Mishnah* was to articulate this sense of inviolate boundary rights; that corpus constructed a precise code that incorporated the unique privileges pertaining to each domain and elaborated on the separate modes whereby the principal instruments of each attained high office. But those early rabbinic regulations, although undoubtedly more specific than any to be found in the Bible itself, were not entirely innovative. *Mishnah* and Scripture did certainly possess somewhat different perspectives on matters appertaining to government.[14] Nevertheless, the lines of continuity between the two bodies of text were strong enough to underscore their similarities. Both enunciate a commitment to the preservation of the independence of governmental franchises whose distinctions had been ordained as early as the dawn of Jewish constitutional development.

Quite obviously at odds with the centralized practice prevalent throughout the ancient Middle East itself, the tripartite structure described in the Bible is also markedly different in purpose from the types of power-diffusion proposed in antiquity by the seminal works of Greek and Roman political analysis. In enumerating the merits of "mixed constitutions," Thucydides, Plato, Aristotle, and Polybius (to name only the most prominent figures cited in the conventional pantheons) sought principally to attain political stability—and the judicial independence upon which that stability was considered to rest.[15] "Substantial interests," they taught, could only be protected from governmental encroachment by institutional arrangements that discriminated against various existing (usually social) agents of strength and that shared out clearly defined (usually functional) areas of governmental prerogatives. It is the fact that the Bible's purposes are different that lends its notions of power-sharing their distinctive character. What distinguishes its paradigm is the primacy it places on the sources of instrumental sovereignties and the purposes of the authorities that they wield. Only secondarily is its division among kings, priests, and prophets designed to reflect the realia of power or to demarcate instrumental boundaries of a functional nature.

In a very specific sense, this aspect of biblical doctrine found expression in the relationship which it ordained between the three demarcated regimes. Their independence did not intimate that they were altogether to be separate. If anything, the Bible stresses that they are to be regarded as interdependent entities. The fact that all three offices derive their divine mandate from precisely parallel processes of covenant merely stresses the extent to which each deserves to be regarded as an equally authoritative mediating instrument between God and His people. It also emphasizes the teaching that they together constitute the sinews of prescribed biblical government. Scripture will not consider any polity to be constitutionally complete unless and until it contains fully functioning representatives in all three franchises. Each has a corporate share in the governance of the body politic through institutions and officers empowered by it. That, to cite but one instance, is why the joint presence of priests, prophets, and (prospective) kings is required at such moments of supreme constitutional importance as the inauguration of a new regime (I Kings 1:38 and II Kings 23:2).

Moreover, while the immediate manifestations of the triptych are immediately apparent, the Bible clearly wishes each of its constituent parts to be seen in its larger significance as well. That, certainly, was the early rabbinic understanding, which regarded each of the individual title-holders as the human incarnation of a distinct governmental domain. *Mishnah* (*Avot* 4:13), for instance, refers to precisely the same triad when speaking of the existence of three *ketarim* (crowns): those of the *torah*, the *kehunah* (priesthood), and the *malkhut* (kingship). *Talmud Bavli* (*Yoma* 72b), in a play on Exodus 25:11; 25:24; 30:3, designates the same clusters as *zeirin* (garlands; see also Rashi's commentary on those verses). Although important, the difference in terminology does not affect the impact of the division.[16] In both texts, kings, priests, and prophets are regarded not as transient individual personalities, but as permanent symbols of biblical political authority, each in possession of distinct prerogatives there laid down in fragmentary sets of law-making enunciations. *Nevi'im*, thus, quite apart from being men individually inspired, are also the generic human means whereby God's teachings to Israel are interpreted, specified, and given concrete expression. *Kohanim*, similarly, are the conduits whereby God and His chosen people are brought into constant contact and close proximity through shared rituals and symbolic expressions. *Melakhim*, finally, incorporate the legitimately empowered means whereby civil relationships within the polity are structured and regulated in accordance with the covenantal stipulations of the divinely ordained constitution. Since the correct ordering of Jewish public life demands expression in all three of these areas, the cooperation of their separate representatives is an essential ingredient of the correct workings of the Jewish governmental system in its entirety. The implication is that the proper biblical polity is one that contains fully articulated representatives in all three domains, and one in which, furthermore, the balance between them is both buttressed and respected.

Political Theory and Political Practice

As the biblical record itself admits, the course of ancient Israel's political history rarely obliged by conforming to such neat categorization. Consequently, attested heights of constitutional perfection—as here outlined—rarely obtained. After an initial phase of gestation (lasting throughout the period of Moses, Joshua, and the sequence of Judges), the three designated branches of government settled into a fairly regular mold. Indeed, the system as a whole seems to have achieved a degree of stability during what is usually designated the first Commonwealth. As the second book of Samuel and both books of Kings and Chronicles illustrate, kings, priests, and prophets then became permanent features of Israelite society, both northern and southern. Nevertheless, and as the same sources reveal, periods of equilibrium between these officers were few and far between. One possible instance is provided by events during the early stages of the united monarchy, when the Davidic kingship became an established fact of Israelite political life but not yet an overweening influence over Israel's political development. Another might be discerned at the very close of the biblical chronicle, when the Ezra–Nehemiah covenant laid down new ground rules for constitutional expression after the restoration in circumstances that necessitated a high degree of interinstitutional cooperation.

But even thus to identify brief moments of apparent constitutional equipoise is to demonstrate the extent to which—even in the biblical phase of Jewish history—they were exceptional. The predominant picture to emerge from the texts is far more turbulent and—for precisely that reason—far more interesting. For the most part, ancient Israel's constitutional history seems to have been shot through with the record of continuous tensions among kings, priests, and prophets (and their respective fellow-travelers). Few of the dramatis personae who carried those titles adhered strictly to the prescribed boundaries of their separate domains; the more colorful among them, especially when the color was laced with charisma, sought to obtain a preponderance of political power and the preeminence of their own particular facet of constitutional interpretation.

To suggest that such conflicts form part of a wider pattern is not, of course, to ignore the unique circumstances by which each was generated. Nevertheless, once attention is shifted from an examination of the immediate motives of particular political episodes to an analysis of their underlying structure, a recurrent pattern does seem to emerge. For all the vicissitudes of ancient Israel's public life, its basic structure appears to conform with remarkable consistency to what can be discerned as clearly defined parameters. Periods of relative constitutional stability, characterized by the maintenance of a king–priest–prophet balance of power, were succeeded by moments of constitutional crisis. The latter occurred when one segment of the triad harnessed sufficient strength to compel a readjustment of the alignment in its entirety. Sooner or later, however, that readjustment was in turn tried and tested. If incapable of resisting the aggrandizement of one or both of the other branches, it was itself superseded by a new constellation of the forces.

If the resilience of this somewhat cyclical pattern is to be understood, note must be taken of the bounds of constitutional propriety within which such periodic gyrations occurred. Even at moments of the greatest antagonism between some or all of the three domains, none of them explicitly challenged the right of the other(s) to a rightful place in the constitutional spectrum of which they all formed a part. Individual prophets, priests, and kings were certainly challenged and deposed (sometimes brutally so); but the realms of prophecy, priesthood, and kingship—as such—were not themselves explicitly denied. At a systemic level, the preferred tactic seems to have been the more benign method of attempted co-option. Principal instruments in one of the franchises attempted (sometimes, and for limited periods, successfully so) to attain commanding authority throughout the polity by posing as the repository of two of the three domains. They thus amalgamated prerogatives that ought properly to have been separated and, as it were, simultaneously wore two crowns. In so doing, they contrived to isolate the third domain, thereby neutralizing its constitutional influence and subjecting it to their own particular will.

Power Struggles in the Constitutional Triad

The historical circumstances that gave rise to such shifts in the balance of constitutional power can be variously categorized. In some (isolated) instances, the biblical texts indicate that a degree of imbalance must be attributed to God's own will. Exercising all the rights of a *deus ex machina*, it was He who determined that—for reasons known only to Himself—the ordained equilibrium of the triad could not be sustained. One outstanding example of a violation thus divinely instigated is provided by the biography of Moses. Invested with the distinctive title of *eved adonai* (servant of the Lord; i.e., His chief minister), Moses, according to the biblical account, received from God a plenitude of extraordinary power embracing all three domains. In practice, if not in name, Moses himself functioned as both *melekh* and *navi*; his brother he installed as *kohen*. As Korach very soon grasped (Numb. 16:3), thus entrenched, the unilateral sovereignty available to Moses seemed to break all the rules of a balanced constitution; his elevated position, indeed, seemed to be dangerously awesome.[17]

In a second category of cases, changes in the balance of power among the three agencies are less directly attributed to divine action. Instead, God is said to work through human (sometimes gentile) instruments. Such was the case, most explicitly, at the time of the destruction of the southern kingdom of Judah. Within the context of the present argument, the Bible's depiction of the causes of that particular catastrophe are not of central concern (although it is essential to note, *en passant*, that the covenantal motif is throughout predominant: exile is the result of Israel's failure to observe the covenant; redemption will signify God's own restoration of that partnership). More relevant are its consequences. The fall of Jerusalem, although undoubtedly a political and cultic calamity, did not automatically terminate the traditional governmental structure. At the most basic level of redemptive aspirations, *nevi'im*, *kohanim*, and even *melakhim* all retained their classic constitutional status. Even though the latter two offices were momentarily deprived of a functional means of expression, they continued to be considered integral components of any future restoration (see, for example, Zechariah's prophecy respecting the *atarot* [crowns]; 6:11). What had changed as a result of the Babylonian captivity, however, was the balance of relationships among the three offices. It was now the domain of prophecy, which during the first commonwealth had been largely subordinated to those of monarchy and priesthood, that increasingly began to exert predominant sway. One indication is provided by Ezekiel's deliberate use of the term *nasi* (prince—and not, one notes, *melekh*) to describe the principal instrument of civil government; another might be found in the fact that it was he (rather than an official spokesman for the priestly domain) who specified the conditions under which the cultic service would be resumed.[18] Ezra's reforms merely consummated the process, extending it to include the reconstitution of the polity on lines that stressed the supremacy of the *sofer* (scribe) as the ultimate interpreter of constitutional doctrine and practice. Indeed, it is probably indicative of the change in the alignment among the three domains that Ezra, although himself of priestly descent, seems to have made very little political use of that fact. Significantly, he preferred to exercise his authority from the alternative bases of the *torah* and—together with Nehemiah—of the civil rulership.[19]

Even more arresting, however, is a third category of constitutional usurpation, which the biblical texts do not attribute to the pressure of external events or agencies, but to the inner workings of the triad itself. In these cases, relations among the three branches alter in response to changes within one of them. Transformations occur, therefore, when individual representatives of a particular domain reinterpret the entire constitution. By formulating policies and programs that deny the very principle of a co-ordinate status for kings, priests, and prophets, they provoke and promote a radically new structure of power. In this way, the two processes—changes within individual domains and changes between them—become entwined. In fact, they feed upon each other, and thus generate chronic tensions at all levels of the polity.

Unquestionably the most explicit biblical examples of this development are provided by the turbulent history of ancient Israel's monarchy. Altogether, indeed, the books of Kings and Chronicles can be read as an extended discourse on the Jewish people's earliest attempts to retain the divinely ordained equilibrium of government in the face of the functional problems imposed by the emergence of a unified center of monarchical power. The process, as described in the texts, was discreetly evolutionary in character. Initially, and possibly as a result of the ingrained tradition of balance, each party to the triad felt the need to proceed with caution. Hence, the reign of Saul (notwithstanding Samuel's earlier forebodings) did not witness the emergence of a dictatorial monarchy. Even if the new sovereign did harbor extensive ambitions (and if so, the Bible does not reveal what they were), publicly he seems to have adopted a relatively moderate course. Throughout his reign, the balance among the three principal domains of government remained fairly stable. Significantly, Saul's own formal title was, initially (I Sam. 9:16; 10:1), *nagid* (one made great) rather than *melekh*, a fact that underscores the limitations on his role. Indeed, the canonical chronicle of his reign throughout stresses the degree to which Saul continued to be trammeled by the contending pressures of franchises that laid claim to bases of quite independent authority.

The most outstanding example of such pressures is provided by the record of relationships between Saul and Samuel, whose retention of the distinctive title of *ro'eh* (seer) was unaffected by the change of regime. From the very inception of the monarchy, Samuel showed himself prepared to pester his new ruler, exercising to the utmost the prophet's inherent constitutional right to review every aspect of national policy—military, judicial, and sacerdotal. Eventually, he even went to the ultimate length of civil disobedience, when appointing (and anointing) a pretender to the throne.[20] This was a challenge to the monarchical prerogative that no ruler could possibly tolerate. But the fact that priests (as at Nob; I Sam. chaps. 21–22) were party to at least one of David's rebellions serves further to emphasize the enormity of Saul's political problem. Indeed, perhaps one of the several biblical lessons of Saul's unhappy reign is that no kingship is secure unless assured of the support of at least one of the other two principal arms of designated constitutional government. Their combined opposition (especially if unified under the direction of a figure as blatantly ambitious as was David) is bound to place the monarchy in a position of intolerable isolation, thereby precluding all possibility of stable government.

As the biblical account shows, the lesson was not lost on Saul's successors, and especially not on Solomon. The latter is portrayed in the texts as (among other things) the very epitome of a thrust toward monarchical aggrandizement. As much is apparent from the magnificence of his court and the multiplicity of his household. It is also illustrated by his reorganization of his realm in a manner designed to undermine the tribal structure and clannish loyalties that his father had alternately exploited and decried.[21] Undoubtedly the most critical of all Solomon's moves, however, especially from the constitutional perspective presented here, was the construction of the Temple. By any standards, this was a masterly stroke, worthy indeed, if not of the "wisest of all men," then certainly of an acute politician. From the moment of its royal dedication (and I Kings 8 leaves no room for doubt as to who was the master of ceremonies at that particular event!), the building entirely changed the balance of traditional governmental forces.

What compounds the achievement is that the realignment occurred without recourse to the use of force, and with no loss of life whatsoever (contrast the unfortunate demise of Uzzah while David was transferring the ark to Jerusalem; II Sam. 6:6–7). Unlike Saul, Solomon did not enter into direct confrontation with the priestly class; unlike David, neither did he attempt to encroach upon their domain by bestowing on his own sons sacerdotal titles to which they were not genetically entitled (which seems to be the import of the otherwise obscure reference in II Sam. 8:18).[22] Rather, and with far more subtlety, he was content merely to subordinate the *kohanim* to his own will, leaving them with but the shadow of their former independence. Within the new and permanent shrine, he afforded them unprecedented opportunities for the flamboyant display of the full panoply of priestly ceremonial, in all its solemnity, mystery, and majesty. Beyond its confines, however, he drastically curtailed their opportunities for the exercise of autonomous political influence. To all intents and purposes, *kohanim* were reduced to honorific spectators on the political stage. Their income, although now assured (and doubtless considerable), was essentially dependent on the maintenance of the edifice built at royal initiative and expense.[23] Hence (and as the bureaucratic lists in Kings and Chronicles bear witness), in name as well as in fact, *kohanim* now constituted little more than the king's own servants.[24]

With the ordained constitutional equilibrium altogether upset by the aggrandizement of one of the three branches of government, the responses of the weakened members of the triad deserve particular attention. If the Old Testament's record of the priesthood is anything to go by,[25] the principal counsel of the biblical texts is for a policy of almost unlimited patience and restraint on the part of the domain whose independence has been curtailed by the ambitions of its more powerful counterpart. To put matters another way, there is no hint in the Bible that the priests should have sought to recapture their former status by a resort to the use of brute force.

One reason (perhaps too obvious to be stated explicitly) is that such a course would have required *kohanim* somehow to overcome the deterrent influence exerted by the brooding presence in Jerusalem of a standing army of royal cohorts. But another, equally important, is that the priesthood—as a governmental agency—was not the domain whose constitutional prerogative it was to employ those means (Zech. 4:6). Far more in keeping with the Bible's rules of the constitutional game was the reliance on divine intervention. That agency could be supremely efficacious (witness the exquisite timing of the attack of leprosy that struck King Uzziah when he insisted on performing a sacerdotal function properly reserved to the priesthood; II Chron. 25:16–21). It was also the most appropriate for a reaffirmation of the priests' rights to be considered an independent branch of Israelite government, and thus for a reassertion of the power-sharing principle. Ultimately, the texts indicate, God would Himself generate fissures in the cohesiveness of the royal domain and thereby provide the priesthood with a chance to play a corporate role commensurate with its status.

That such opportunities could indeed occur was indicated by at least two incidents in Judean history. The first occurred during the bloody rule of Athaliah, against whom Jehoiada the priest led popular opposition. By restoring the throne to Joash, inaugurating a new covenant between "God, the king, and the people," and resanctifying the sanctuary (in that order; II Kings chaps. 11–12 and II Chron. chaps. 23–24), Jehoiada accomplished far more than a successful palace revolt or religious reformation. He also demonstrated the extent to which it was still possible to reassert the rightful constitutional authority of the entire priestly domain. The lesson, clearly, was not lost on Hilkiah, who played an equally crucial role in the halcyon days of Josiah's far-reaching reforms. Indeed, the biblical depiction of that program (II Kings chaps. 22–23) contains two further points of interest: at their inception, the reforms were sanctioned by representatives of all three domains (as indicated by the consultation among Hilkiah, Josiah, and Hulda the prophetess; II Kings 22:3–20); during its course Hilkiah became the first individual to whom the title of *kohen gadol* was explicitly appended (cf. e.g., II Kings 22:4,8 and 23:4 with the anonymous use in Numb. 35:25; Josh. 20:6, and even II Kings 12:11).

Even more interesting, however, is the reaction of the third base of the triad—that which feels itself to be placed in a position of dangerous isolation by the combined forces of the other two. Throughout most of the period of the first commonwealth, the domain of prophecy was thus situated as a result of the domination that the monarchy exerted over the priesthood and its representatives, who, accordingly, were forced to search for a means of redress. Thus analyzed, Samuel's initial opposition to the very notion of a hereditary monarchy assumes a new layer of meaning. I Sam. 8:11–18 does not merely articulate the traditional opposition of an advocate of direct divine rule to the prospect of a ruthless human monarchy; rather, it ought perhaps to be read as a highly partisan *cri de coeur*, emanating from a representative of the branch of government most likely to be weakened as a result of the proposed initiative. In thus advocating a policy of conservatism, Samuel was—from the perspective of his own domain—in fact adopting a strategy of entrenchment. His object was to contain the new monarchy within the bounds of the old order and to prevent it from assuming the position of priority afforded by popular pressure.[26]

Notwithstanding Samuel's own efforts, the strategy he advocated was essentially forlorn. Under the circumstances created by the new monarchy, prophets could not continue to assert their former independence simply by clinging with gritty determination to institutions and procedures that were fast becoming outdated. Admittedly, the domain that they represented did remain an integral component of the constitutional process, especially at its more dramatic moments. Nathan played a crucial role in the palace intrigues that preceded the designation of Solomon as successor to David (I Kings chap. 1); Ahijah the Shilonite bestowed prior divine sanction on the secessionist ambitions of Jeroboam (I Kings 11:29–39); at Elisha's command, Jehu was anointed King of Israel during Joram's reign (II Kings 9:1ff). But these intrusions, although themselves critical, were still a far cry from the continuous role to which the domain was constitutionally entitled and to which it had become accustomed under Samuel's stewardship. Particularly instructive, in this connection, is a comparison between Samuel's reaction to Saul's failure to exact precise retribution from the Amalekites (I Sam. 15:2–35) and Nathan's response to the awful manner in which David disposed of Uriah the Hittite (II Sam. 11:2–12:25). The former occasioned a brutally blunt diatribe during the course of which the prophet publicly shamed his king; the latter resulted in little more than an intimate *tête-à-tête*, better remembered for the parable to which it gave rise than for the heinous crime by which it was occasioned.[27]

Given this state of affairs, a more drastic course was ultimately required. Prophets could not retain their autonomy simply by working within the political system now dominated by the monarch; they had to attack it from without. That, indeed, was the policy pungently adopted by Elijah, Elishah, Amos, Isaiah, Hosea, Micah, and Jeremiah. All posed as the repositories of the moral conscience of Israel, not least by adumbrating a distinct "prophetic code" whose claims to authority resided in their own highly personal experiences of direct divine revelation. All, accordingly, refused to have anything to do with the methods and policies advocated and adopted by the various circles of "court seers" dismissively termed *nevi'ei ha-sheker* (false prophets). Rather, and in a possible attempt to strengthen their position, some sought to benefit from the advantages attendant on the foundation of a crude bureaucratic infrastructure. By establishing "schools" of followers,[28]

they even initiated procedures of institutional succession and entitle-
ment (e.g., II Kings 9:1–6) reminiscent of those originally appertaining
solely to the monarchy and the priesthood. In accomplishing all of this,
they were not only fostering an *esprit de corps*, nor even attempting to
moderate the more extreme manifestations of royal dictatorship in a series
of sublime messages of warning and/or comfort; they were also making
an essentially political statement. By thus claiming the authority to evaluate the performance of the kings and priests by the standards of the *torat
mosheh* (and their atavistic invocation of that constitutional referent, as in
Malachi 3:22, was surely politically motivated), they were both expanding
the effective arc of their own domain and contracting that of their constitutional competitors. Thus perceived, indeed, their activities constituted an
assault on the very idea that the monarchy, in its contemporary guise, was
truly deserving of Israel's loyalties.

Whether or not that theme ultimately underlies the record of
Jeremiah's incitement to civil disobedience is debatable.[29] What does
appear undeniable is the revolutionary implication of the "new covenant" (e.g., Jer. 31:30ff; cf. Malachi 2:4–8). Indeed, the central thrust
of that document is the primacy of prophetic instruction—above all
other instruments of government—in a regime committed to the pursuit of social justice and to the attainment of a more immediate relationship with God than either priests or kings were prepared to allow
(see also the exchange recorded in Amos 7:10–17). These developments, then, were far more than the reflexive reactions of charismatic
spokesmen for popular resistance to royal absolutism (though they
were that too). They were, perhaps above all, attempts to repair in-
fringements of the divinely ordained balance of constitutional power
among the three domains. By the invention and application of new
mechanisms and programs, the prophets aspired to restore some balance to the political structure that they deemed to have been undermined by the combined actions of kings and priests.

Conclusion

To regard such episodes as individual phases in a stream of political
intrigue is not to deny the underlying religious impulse of the biblical
texts. If anything, that reading might serve to emphasize the extent to
which scripture posits an interaction between the sacred and the secular elements of human endeavor, insisting on the virtues of a system of
government that encompasses both domains of public life. Political

action in the public arena, it teaches, is in no way to be regarded as divorced from religious behavior. On the contrary, in properly constituted regimes, various forms of political power could attain sacred status. When duly commissioned and exercised, human rulership constitutes an essential ingredient in the construction of God's own holy commonwealth on earth.

If they were to fulfill that mandate, human authorities obviously had to act justly and in righteousness. This, however, was not perceived to be merely a personal requirement; it was also a systemic ordinance. Government, in other words, had itself to be structured and organized in a manner that might preclude tyranny and facilitate the communal attainment of good conduct in the manifold realms of human expression.

This chapter has attempted to analyze the implications and manifestations of that teaching. Concentrating on the structure of biblical political dialogues, it has sought to discern the underlying mold within which they were cast and took place. When studied synoptically, the various incidents portrayed in the Old Testament do provide evidence for a biblical definition of the proper mode of political conduct and the appropriate form of governmental organization. Whatever the unique characteristics the several biblical depictions of political conflict in ancient Israel, their underlying import is a remarkably consistent scriptural preference for a distinct framework of power-sharing. Indeed, it is the existence of that framework which confers coherence on several seemingly disparate elements of ancient Israel's constitutional history, enabling the reader of the texts to integrate them into a recognizable pattern of political theory and practice.

Thus perceived, the biblical insistence on power-sharing constitutes far more than a mere nod in the direction of the principle of representative government. This unique tripartite division of authority reflects, in a very subtle way, the multifaceted and interlocking character of the text's theopolitical thrust. At the same time, the paradigm illustrates the measure of scripture's normative commitment to a constitutional form of power-sharing that might complement its own covenantal and republican principles. Demarcating the franchises represented by kings, priests, and prophets are neither conflicting bases of material power (as was commonly depicted in classical political theory) nor artificially cocooned differences of function (as was to be posited, in different forms, by medieval Christian lawyers and modern constitutional theorists), but rather more subtle distinctions of orientation. Although independent, they are not portrayed as severely compartmentalized spheres of jurisdiction with one (or more) being responsible for matters secular and the other (or others) for matters religious. On the contrary, what characterizes the Old Testament's system of power-sharing here portrayed, indeed what transposes it into a *system*, is the interdependence of the relationship between its constituent parts. In the biblical scheme of things, kings, priests, and prophets are regarded as joint partners in the entire business of government—judicial as well as executive, military as well as civil, lay as well as sacerdotal. In every one of these arenas of public life, each of the officers is entitled to act as a particular prism on the compound constitution of the polity and to preserve its integrity. Indeed, their differentiation is designed to facilitate the attainment of that goal. Power-sharing among them is not a consequence of either an inability to resolve conflicts over sovereignty or a search for administrative equity. It manifests a philosophical commitment to a disposition of political authority which, through the choreography of reciprocal constitutional action, is designed to teach humans how to live lives that are good and holy.

As is the case with other biblical teachings, the influence of the king-priest–prophet relationship described in the Old Testament persisted far beyond the closure of the scriptural canon. As distilled by early rabbinic literature, the biblical concept of power-sharing became an integral facet of the Jewish political tradition in its entirety. Its impact on Western political philosophy, although less direct, was equally pervasive. Admittedly, Gelasius and John of Salisbury considerably refracted the notion when positing (with reference to Matthew 22:21) the two "swords" of Christian rulership; Montesquieu subjected it to even more radical reinterpretation when making famous a normative system of checks and balances among the three "branches" of modern government. But even when thus modifying the form that a separation of powers might take, neither of those traditions could deny the cardinality with which it had earlier been invested in the biblical sources. Notional adherence to that principle survived several cultural watersheds and political revolutions.[30] Becoming widespread, and in some cases obsessional, it exerted a conceptual impact that helped to shape the very texture of the history and culture of the entire Western world.

Notes

1. D.J. Elazar, "Government in Biblical Israel," *Tradition*, 8 (1968): 106. Although what follows is sometimes at odds with several of Elazar's conclusions, my debt to his approach is nevertheless substantial. For an introduction to some of the ideas developed here, see our joint work: D.J. Elazar and S.A. Cohen, *The*

Jewish Polity: Jewish Political Organization from Biblical Times to the Present (Bloomington: Indiana University Press, 1985), esp. chaps. 1–5. For examples of an alternative approach see P. Ramsay, "Elements of Biblical Political Theory," *Journal of Religion*, 29 (1949): 258–83

2. That is not to ignore, of course, the degree to which precisely that notion is present. The biblical view is graphically portrayed in such texts as Psalms 97; the rabbinical perspective is summarized in the *Tanhuma* pericope cited by Rashi in his first commentary on the book of Genesis.

3. For a concise summary of the conventional materials see *Entsiklopedia Mikrait*, vol. 4 (Jerusalem: Massada, 1962), clmns. 1118–28; also J. Gray, "Kingship of God in Prophets and Psalms," *Vetus Testamentum*, 11 (1961): 1–29. A detailed exposition of the implications of the notion in Martin Buber's classic work, *The Kingship of God* (New York: Harper and Row, 1967).

4. For a summary of the scholarly debate on the presence or absence of a notion of sacral kingship in ancient Israel see: A.R. Johnson, *Sacral Kingship in Ancient Israel*, 2d ed. (Cardiff: University of Wales Press, 1967).

5. See Buber, *Kingship of God*, pp. 59–65. Nevertheless, Gideon's position may not have been dictated entirely by altruism; on the contrary, he may have been aiming at precisely the sort of uncontested power that only God, and not the populace, could bestow. See B. Lindars, "Gideon and Kingship," *Journal of Theological Studies*, 16 (1965): 315–26.

6. For analyses of this seminal concept, see L. Perlitt, *Bundestheologie im Alten Testament* (Cologne: Neukirschen-Vluyn, 1961); and D.J. McCarthy, *Treaty and Covenant*, rev. ed. (Rome: Pontifical Biblical Institute, 1977); and, on the specifically political ramifications in their Jewish historical setting, biblical and postbiblical, D.J. Elazar, "Covenant as the Basis of the Jewish Political Tradition," in *Kinship and Consent: The Jewish Political Tradition and Its Contemporary Uses*, ed. D.J. Elazar (Ramat Gan: Turtledove, 1981), chap. 1.

7. K.D. Sakenfeld, *The Meaning of Hesed in the Hebrew Bible*, Harvard Semitic Monographs, 17 (Missoula: Scholars Press, 1978).

8. J. Weingreen, *From Bible to Mishna* (Manchester: Manchester University Press, 1976), pp. 109–10; and G. Ostbron, *Tora in the Old Testament* (Uppsala: Uppsala University Arsskrift, 1957).

9. The theme of communal responsibility and mutual rights pervades much of early rabbinic literature. For a summary of the limitations it imposes on governing elites, rabbis as well as laymen, see S. Schechter, *Some Aspects of Rabbinic Theology* (New York: Jewish Publication Society of America, 1923); and, more recently, M. Elon, *Ha-mishpat ha-Ivri: Toldotav, Mekorotav, Ekronatav* (Jerusalem: Magnes Press, 1973). The concept of an ongoing covenant is expounded in Deut. 29:9–14.

10. Particularly notable are those passages that describe the confederated framework of Israel's early tribal system and the acclamatory—sometimes consultative—role of the "people" in later periods. For discussions of these phenomena, stressing their essentially "democratic" implications, see, for example, R. Gordis, "Democratic Origins in Ancient Israel—The Biblical Edah," in *Alexander Marx Jubilee Volume*, ed. S. Lieberman (New York: Jewish Theological Seminary, 1950), pp. 369–88; and R. de Vaux, "Le sens de l'expression 'peuple du pays' dans l'Ancient Testament et le rôle politique du peuple en Israël," *Revue d'Assyriologie*, 58 (1964): 167–72.

11. That is why Abram can invoke jurisprudential principles when haggling

over the fate of Sodom (Genesis 18:25); and Moses can refer to basic rights when attempting to avert God's wrath from the children of Israel (Numbers 16:22).

12. That, certainly, is the plain meaning of the text. It has to be noted, however, that later traditions were unable to resist the temptation to attribute to Moses a plenitude of constitutional powers not granted to him in the Bible itself. Philo, for instance, describes him as Israel's "captain and leader the High Priest and prophet and friend of God," *De Sacrificiis Abelis et Caini*, IV, 130. Talmudic sources, although arguably more precise, are only marginally less extravagant. They entitle him both "king and prophet"; for example, TB *Shavu'ot* 15a. The most recent attempt to assess Moses's political importance, although stressing the wide range of his powers, does not explicitly address the degree to which he concentrated constitutional power in his own hands. See A. Wildavsky, *The Nursing Father: Moses As a Political Leader* (Tuscaloosa: University of Alabama Press, 1985); cf. C. Hauret, "Moïse etait-il prêtre?" *Analecta biblica*, 10 (1959): 375–87; and J.R. Porter, *Moses and Monarchy* (Oxford: Basil Blackwell, 1963).

13. See also the juxtapositions in Jer. 33:17–22; II Chron. 13:4–11, and Ecclesiasticus 45:24–25; in general, A.H.J. Gunneweg, "Sinaibund und Davidsbund," *Vetus Testamentum*, 10 (1960): 335ff. On the extent to which the royal covenants may be considered conditional, see J. Liver, *Toldot Bet David* (Jerusalem: Magnes, 1959), pp. 63–66; and F.M. Cross, *Canaanite Myth and Hebrew Epic* (Cambridge: Harvard University Press, 1973), pp. 219–65.

14. As is argued by J. Neusner, "Scriptural, Essenic and Mishnaic Approaches to Civil Law and Government: Some Comparative Remarks," *Harvard Theological Review*, 73 (1980): 419–34.

15. For discussions of classical approaches to "mixed constitutions" see C.H. McIlwain, *Constitutionalism: Ancient and Modern* (Ithaca: Cornell University Press, 1947), pp. 33–35; F.W. Walbank, *Polybius* (Berkeley: University of California Press, 1972), pp. 135, 149–56; and F.D.Wormuth, *The Origins of Modern Constitutionalism* (New York: Kennikat Press, 1949), chaps. 1, 4, and 8. For analyses of the ancient Egyptian, Mesopotamian, and Hittite regimes, see the articles by J.A. Wilson, E.A. Speiser, and H.G. Guterbock, in "Authority and Law in the Ancient Orient," *Journal of the American Oriental Society*, supplement no. 17 (1954).

16. I have addressed this question at greater length in my article "The Concept of the Three *ketarim*: Its Place in Jewish Political Thought and Its Implications for a Study of Jewish Political History," *Association for Jewish Studies Review*, 9 (1984): 27–54.

17. For early rabbinic views on the meaning of the title *eved adonai*, see *Sifrei* to Deut. chap. 27 (ed. Finkelstein, pp. 42–43). Recent interpretations are summarized in S. Mowinkel, *He That Cometh* (Oxford: Basil Blackwell, 1954), pp. 187–257. Significantly, aggadic discussions of the public motives of Korach's rebellion stress that the separation of powers was an essential plank in his platform. See M. Ber, "Meridat Korah umenieihah be-agadot hazal," *Mekhkarim . . . lezekher Yosef Heinemann*, ed. A. Fleischer et al. (Jerusalem: Magnes, 1981), pp. 9–33.

18. See, in general, C.R. North, "The Old Testament Estimate of the Monarchy," *American Journal of Semitic Languages and Literature*, 48 (1931–32): 1–19; and Liver, *Toldot Beit David*, pp. 102–3.

19. In this connection, two further points are worthy of note. One is the degree

to which Nehemiah was a party to this program; indeed, according to one interpretation, he may even have harbored ambitions of a more extreme nature, attempting to utilize the extraordinary powers conferred upon him by the Persian overlord to assume himself the position of kingship otherwise denied him by his inappropriate genealogical antecedents. See A.L. Ivry, "Nehemiah 6:10: Politics and the Temple," *Journal for the Study of Judaism*, 3 (1972): 35–45; the other is the early rabbinic bias toward Ezra, displayed in the talmudic parallel drawn between him, as the chief representative of the domain of the *torah*, and Moses. See *Tosefta, Sanhedrin* 4:7.

20. For a politically slanted interpretation, emphasizing—and perhaps exaggerating—Samuel's priestly affiliations, see M.A. Cohen, "The Role of the Shilonite Priesthood in the United Monarchy of Ancient Israel," *Hebrew Union College Annual*, 36 (1965), esp. pp. 69–70. On Samuel's title, see H.M. Orlinsky, "The Seer in Ancient Israel," *Oriens Antiquas*, 1965.

21. Examples such as this underscore the need for a rigorous lexicon of specifically political terms to be found in the Bible. Such a compilation would prove particularly useful in highlighting the appearance of the term *nitzavim* in I Kings 4:7–14. Originally applied to non-Israelite administrations (II Sam. 8:6), it was adopted for Israelite use by Solomon in a blatant attempt to rule through the agency of territorial *intendants* of his own choice, rather than through the traditional framework provided by the tribal structure. Note, too, the administrative changes initiated by a later exemplar of royal absolutism, Ahab, in whose reign mention is first made of *medinot* (states; I Kings 20:14), regional divisions similarly intended to supersede tribes.

22. For early rabbinic attempts to wriggle out of this difficulty, see the translation of this verse attributed to Yonatan ben Uzziel.

23. T. Ishida, *The Royal Dynasties in Ancient Israel* (Berlin: W. de Gruyter, 1977), pp. 142–43. Of course, even in Jerusalem, the construction of the Temple merely culminated a process; it did not stand in isolation. Solomon's blunt deposition of Abiathar (I Kings 2:26), an event that was to cause several rabbinical constitutionalists later to shuffle their feet in embarrassment (TB *Sotah* 45b), had already indicated the direction in which the wind was likely to blow. See A. Alt, "Formation of the Israelite State in Palestine," in *Essays on Old Testament History and Religion* (Oxford: Basil Blackwell, 1960), p. 218 and fn. 17; Y. Aharoni, *The Land of the Bible* (London: Allen and Unwin, 1966), pp. 268–73; and E.W. Heaton, *Solomon's New Men: The Emergence of Ancient Israel as a Nation State* (London: Thames and Hudson, 1974), pp. 50–51.

24. This was especially the case in the northern kingdom, after the secession. There, as is pointed out in I Kings 12:31, Jeroboam went as far as to disregard altogether hereditary criteria for priestly appointments. But a recurrence of the pattern may have been contemplated at the restoration. Zech. 4:9 and 6:12–13 certainly intimates that the new sanctuary was to be constructed by Zerubabel. See B. Halpern, *The Constitution of the Monarchy in Israel* (Missoula: Scholars Press, 1981), p.27ff.

25. Perhaps the most interesting account of the Old Testament priesthood, stressing the political elements in the chronicle, remains that by J. Morgenstern, "A Chapter in the History of the High Priesthood," *American Journal of Semitic Languages and Literature*, 55 (1938): 1–24; 183–97; 360–77. A more recent survey, which stresses the ritualistic components and almost entirely underplays

the political, is M. Haran, *Temple and Temple Service in Ancient Israel* (Oxford: Clarendon Press, 1978).

26. In this connection, particular attention might be paid to Samuel's use of the phrase *mishpat ha-melekh* to describe the constitutional stance to be expected of the prospective monarch. It is difficult to avoid the impression that this is a deliberate echo of Deut. 18:3 and I Sam. 2:12–13 (*mishpat ha-kohanim*), designed to place both the monarchical and priestly domains in a position of subordinate equality to the prophecy. For this, and other observations, I am indebted to Prof. M. Garsiel, of the Bible Department at Bar-Ilan University. See, in general, M. Garsiel, *The First Book of Samuel: A Literary Study of Comparative Structures, Analogies and Parallels* (Ramat Gan: Revivim, 1983). A similar reflection of the same idea might be located in Psalms 96:6, where, intriguingly, Samuel's name is coupled with those of Moses and Aaron. See, on this point, *Talmud Bavli* (TB) *Rosh ha-Shanah* 25a–b and Numbers *Rabbah* 18:8.

27. Limitations of space preclude a full analysis of the agonizing problem that this incident posed for early rabbinic exegesis. What has to be noted, however, is that the sources did acknowledge that a significant change had occurred in the balance between king and prophet. See, e.g., TB *Sanhedrin* 107a and *Sotah* 21a. In general, A. Aptowitzer, "Politikah Hashmona'it ve-neged Hashmona'it be-Halakhah u-ve-Agadah," *Sefer . . . Poznanski*, reprint (Jerusalem: Magnes, 1969), pp. 157–58 and fn. 48, and L. Ginzberg, *Legends of the Jews*, vol. 6 (New York: Jewish Publication Society of America), p. 265, n. 92.

28. For example, the *benei ha-nevi'im* of, e.g., II Kings chap. 2; on whom see J. Muilenberg, "The 'Office' of the Prophet in Ancient Israel," in J.P. Hyatt, ed., *The Bible in Modern Scholarship* (New York: Ktav, 1966), pp. 79–97.

29. The argument is set out in J.A. Wicoxen, "The Political Background of Jeremiah's Temple Sermon," *Rylaarsdam* (1977), pp. 151–66.

30. These later developments are discussed in B. Gwyn, "The Meaning of the Separation of Powers," *Tulane Studies in Political Science*, no. 11 (New Orleans, 1965); F. Dvornik, *Early Christian and Byzantine Political Philosophy: Origins and Background* (Cambridge: Harvard University Press, 1966); E.H. Kantorowicz, *The King's Two Bodies: A Study in Medieval Political Theology* (Princeton: Princeton University Press, 1957); and M.J.C. Vile, *Constitutionalism and the Separation of Powers* (Oxford: Clarendon Press, 1967).

"Ideal" and "Real" in Classical Jewish Political Theory

From the Talmud to Abrabanel

GERALD J. BLIDSTEIN

The relationship of law and political theory to reality—that is, to the actual doings of people in society and to the concrete problems faced by societies—is undoubtedly complex. Are law and political theory to shape reality? Or is the reverse true, and both law and theory are to take their cue from society? This, of course, is a very abstract formulation of the issue. It is also an overly extreme and polarized formulation, for it is likely that the relationship of law and political theory to reality is dynamic and indeed dialectical. But however one refines the formulation, the problem remains. It is often at the heart of vigorous political dispute; it is also high on the scholarly agenda and is treated by both philosophers and historians, as well as by sociologists, anthropologists, and others. These, of course, ask whether the normative statement is borne out in historical reality.

Revealed, divinely inspired law ostensibly need not face this dilemma. Such law, bestowed upon and obliging "all your generations," is assumed to be fundamentally stable, unchanging, perhaps eternal. Authoritative, it is intended to govern its society and shape it in its own image. I am not concerned here with whether neutral historians would accept this description, but rather with how the system looks to its adherents, from "the inside," as it were, and according to its own immanent logic. This logic does not claim that rules and regulations remain identical throughout history. It will argue, however, that variation largely reflects the application of the same unchanging principles and norms in varied circumstances so that the law remains true to itself and its structures, in the deepest sense.

Now, I will grant that this immanent logic of revealed law is a very simplistic description, omitting much and distorting much. But it also contains much that is true. Yet, if this description fits most areas regulated by revealed law, it does not accurately render the career of revealed law in the polity or in governing the political sphere—even from the perspective of that law itself. Here, theorists of the law argue that a "two-tiered system" exists, one that allows and even requires a wide gap between the tiers. In its fullest, medieval formulation, this theory speaks of ideal law for an ideal society and realistic law for a real society. Ideal law is our familiar revealed law, the classical law known in both principles and details, and it is appropriate for an ideal society. Real law, on the other hand, derives its authority from the initial revealed law, but its actual content will be devised so as to guarantee social order in times of disorder—that is to say, in human history as we know it. (Parenthetically, I will note that for both Muslim and Jewish theorists, even ideal man and his society require law, as neither law nor political governance is the product of human corruption.) A pithy expression of this theory was given in fourteenth-century Spain by Solomon ibn Adret (Rashba): ". . . for if you base yourselves on the law of the Torah in this and similar situations . . . the world [i.e., society] would be destroyed."[1]

Modern discussion of Islam has focused sharply (and often unsympathetically) on this postulate of a "two-tiered system," which is quite widespread in classical Islamic political and legal theory. With the development of the Islamic state (and then, states) in the early medieval period, the actual governance of society departed further and further from the pristine rule of Islamic jurisprudence, just as its political structure resembled less and less the normative reality of the first *khalifs*. These phenomena were not castigated by Islamic theorists as violations of the divinely legislated order; rather, they were legitimated as necessary expressions of the "second tier" of the Islamic order itself. Modern scholars have documented the dimensions of the gap between the "ideal" and "real" tiers, and have then proceeded to censure the classical theorists for this "betrayal of the intellectuals," a betrayal tailored to fit the contours of political power in the Islamic state.[2] This legitimation of power despite its opposition to the ideal norms of Islamic life has even been identified as a basic cause of Islamic political demoralization. For revealed law, being divine, can never be repealed or superseded and the rationalization that underlies the "two-tier" theory may explain why the ideal revealed law is not functioning, but it will not successfully convince the believer that his society (and its spiritual leadership) has not betrayed it spiritual commitment.[3]

Talmudic Doctrine

It is difficult to summarize "Talmudic doctrine" on any topic, for this involuted and protean work does not easily lend itself to systematization, and certainly not to generalization and abstraction. Nor did the scholarly tradition inaugurated by the Talmud attempt to reduce its classical forebear to these dimensions; rather, it usually proceeded to apply the concrete Talmudic discussion to other concrete instances. Nonetheless, I shall attempt some generalizations in the light of the problematic of the "ideal" and the "real," focusing on phenomena that may reflect what I have called the "two-tier" theory. These phenomena range from the properly political to the jurisprudential and highlight, as well, the different modalities of "reality" that Jewish history forced its theorists and legists to confront. The structure that enables Talmudic rabbis to retreat from the definitive, "ideal" norms of the Torah is the rabbinic power of legislation (*takkanah*), which implies that the Torah can be "corrected"—expanded or contracted. The "two-tier" theory in the sphere of the political is then simply one expression of a classic and ubiquitous rabbinic device; "*takkanah*" both implies the theory itself and gives it the instrumentality by which it concretizes itself. Now, given the complexities of Talmud literary history, it is likely that other forms also reflect rabbinic revision of the biblical system; scriptural exegesis, for example, often makes rabbinic legislation.[4] But inasmuch as my major interest lies in pinpointing the theory held by the rabbis, I prefer to work on material in which they consciously express their motivation, rather than on texts that are highly opaque to our problem to begin with.

The most dramatic exemplar of the "two-tier" theory does in fact concern the political sphere proper. Biblical anthropology, as it is well known, sees all men as God's creatures, subject to His law. This anthropology produces a system of governance in which no ruler is absolute: the king is to share power with the "elders" or with the Sanhedrin, and he is of course subject to the same law as any other Israelite: "If he violates a positive command or a negative command he is treated as an ordinary individual."[5] But this principled norm crumbled in the face of monarchical power in the early Roman times, when in the aftermath of a confrontation with Alexander Yannai, it was decided that "the king may neither judge nor be judged."[6] The king was thus placed beyond the reach of any humanly effective legal restraint. This surrender to brute power delivered a major blow to the Jewish political tradition, and I do not wish to minimize the force of the laconic Mishnaic regulation. But this retreat from the "ideal" (and it is not a singular retreat, for the nonpolitical sphere offers other examples)[7] is limited in a way characteristic of the entire rabbinic tradition. For if the king is placed beyond the reach of justice—of human justice, that is, for in a traditional culture God was always the final and inescapable judge—he is simultaneously banished from participation in the judicial system. The Talmud claims that this is required by a moral symmetry: one who is not subject to the laws himself cannot judge others. Yet we can also see in this stance the attempt of a system, highly sensitive to the need to separate powers, to limit the power it cannot control. Characteristically, the rabbis attempt to preserve the integrity of the judicial system.

Having opened our discussion of the "two-tiered system" with materials concerning the monarch, it would seem natural to give pride of place to *Mishpat HaMelekh* (the king's law)—the constellation of monarchic powers outlined in I Samuel 8, discussed in the Talmud, and ultimately codified in the medieval collections. But the fact of the matter is that, until medieval times, *Mishpat HaMelekh* is not the overriding category it is sometimes claimed to be, as we shall see. Both the Bible and Talmud apparently understand *Mishpat HaMelekh* as granting the monarch extraordinary powers in the pursuit of matters of state, primarily wars and taxation, as well as in the appropriation of personal servants. But there is little intimation that governance as a whole is beyond the rule of law or that the varied norms obliging the courts and the elders in, say, Exodus 21–22 can be voided. This, at least, is the Maimonidean reading of Bible and Talmud. Others such as the tosafists (and possibly Rashi) did in fact read the matter more broadly and so had difficulty squaring the powers granted the king with, say, Ahab's need to stage a judicial murder in order to gain the vineyard of Naboth. Certainly, the Talmudic debate as to whether *Mishpat Ha-Melekh* itself is a bestowal of legitimate power or, rather, a prophetic warning to Israel of the evil monarchy would bring, is most relevant;

the latter position clearly maintains that there can be no compromise with *any* of the biblical norms of justice even for reasons of state. Yet even if *Mishpat HaMelekh* is accepted as legitimate bestowal, it does not create a systematic, broad alternative to the normative law recognized by Bible and Talmud. Consequently, when this alternative does emerge in medieval theory, we are hard-pressed to exhibit its Talmudic antecedents. This crux is symbolized by the Talmudic (or at least the Babylonian Talmud's) insistence that the Davidic king "is judged," as we have just seen.

The Talmud, of course, is most concerned with courts and what they do; consequently, its major resolutions of the tension between the "ideal" and the "real" are to be found in this sphere. I suggest that we speak of two types or areas of activity. There is first the bestowal of broad prerogative, or discretionary power. Second, there is a controlled relaxation of certain specified provisions of the rule-structure itself.

The parade of examples for the Tannaitic bestowal of discretionary power in extraordinary situations tell of a Jew stoned to death for riding a horse on the Sabbath in Maccabean times, of a lashing administered to a groom who acquired his wife by publicly cohabiting with her, and of eighty witches who were tried and executed on a single day by Simeon b. Shetah. The imposition of more severe penalties than those imposed by the Torah and the suspension of normal procedure are allowed with full recognition that the sinner "is not worthy of such," but that "it is the demand of the hour"; that is to say, historical and social conditions require exemplary and severe punishment "so as to safeguard the Torah."[8] Thus the Talmud explicitly articulates the distinction between the law as appropriate for the isolated individual and the law as an aspect of social governance and formation. (It is possible that the Talmud also allows, under this rubric, suspension of other procedural rules, such as those defining acceptable witnesses, the need for proper warning, and so on.)[9] Now, although this Talmudic doctrine of discretionary powers becomes quite central in medieval theory, as we shall see, I think it played a rather limited role in Talmudic thinking proper, and that it was not a generative structure. There are a small number of instances, located in amoraic Babylonia, that may reflect the doctrine (it is not mentioned specifically),[10] but this ought not to obscure the fact that it does not sustain Talmud discussion or provide a pivotal norm.[11] The Talmud as a whole is much too committed to the rule of law to expound the doctrine of discretionary powers.[12] Indeed, the Talmudic commitment to the law seems to be such that it does not even develop a functioning concept of equity.[13] But judges were allowed (or even expected) to apply statutory law selectively, based on their evaluation of the character and reliability of witnesses and parties to a dispute—which is also a form of discretionary power.[14]

Another, even broader, Talmudic phenomenon can be mentioned here. Talmudic legal analysis will frequently distinguish types of sanctions: some are *kenas*, or "fines," while other payments are designated *mamon* (or *din*), or "compensation." The distinction between these two categories is variously defined, but on some occasions it is clear that *kenas* was levied because the offender was not liable for compensation under Torah law, but the rabbis felt—often for reason of policy—that payment should be made. This, it would seem, embodies some form of a "two-tier" theory, where rabbinic law must accommodate a reality that ideal Torah law need not recognize. Yet it should be pointed out that even where the definition I have used is appropriate, the phenomenon is not necessarily relevant to our discussion, for the Talmud will often assert that even payments provided for in the Torah are *kenas* (e.g., the half-compensation paid by the owner of an innocent [*tam*] goring ox).

On the whole, though, the Talmud moves in another direction when it decides that "reality" is stronger than the situation for which the law was originally devised: it selectively—but universally—relaxes the rules. Here, the major "reality" problems considered are economic pressures and the malfunctioning of the legal system itself in objective historical situations. Thus, witnesses in civil cases will not be subject to the rigorous questioning required by Torah law so as to ease collection of debts, thereby opening credit lines.[15] Significant reconstruction of the rules constitutive of courts is undertaken for similar reasons, when it becomes clear that requiring judges to be fully authorized would reduce the number of operating tribunals to an unacceptable number.[16]

Does the Talmud indeed know the "two-tier" theory expounded at the outset of this paper? The concept is certainly not formulated explicitly. Rabbinic enactments of new rules to supersede the Talmud norms seem to acknowledge the fact that new situations warrant new regulations; but again, it is nowhere stated that the Torah's rules apply to a more "ideal" society or situation than do the rabbinic ones, though the new rabbinic rules are always devised so as to meet a problem that, in theory at least, did not exist for the divine legislator. Talmudic bestowal of discretionary power does seem to imply at the very least that divine law is suited for less threatening times than those for which broad discretionary powers are the proper tactic. But as we have seen, this structure is not especially attractive to the Talmud, which does not seem to base social governance on discretionary prerogative. On the whole, then, the Talmud apparently considers Torah law appropriate to a normal society, with the proviso that extraordinary situations demand more extreme measures. Rather than two broad and distinct categories, we have a spectrum that allows for variety.

Maimonides

Moses Maimonides (1135–1204) massively expands the role of discretionary power in his scheme of political governance. Such power is applied to a far broader range of problems and it is distributed to a larger group of functionaries.[17] The significance of discretionary power for Maimonides is not measured, however, by these quantitative tests alone. Rather, Maimonides seems to take discretionary power as a central aspect of government, a frequently exercised function rather than a highly extraordinary event. In all this—the types of problems resolved by discretionary power, the identity of its wielders, its overall role in the scheme of government and social control—Maimonides's account parallels that of major currents in Islamic law and theory. At the same time, he integrates discretionary power into the more normatively structured scheme of governance in a way that is quite congruent with a specifically Jewish view of the polity, a view that set the limits within which this power must function.

Discretionary power is granted, in the Maimonidean scheme, to the king as well as to the court.[18] It may be possible to infer this from Talmudic materials,[19] but it is more likely that the matter is much more basic and derives from the very heart of Maimonides's political vision. This recaptures something much closer to the biblical structuring of the state in which the king plays the central role in maintaining order. A similar situation exists with regard to the power granted the king to appoint judges (a power shared, of course, with the Great Court); here too one hears the resonance of biblical theory, though Talmudic precedent is not entirely lacking.[20] In both instances the extent of monarchic power over and against that of the court is significantly increased. The reach of discretionary power, it would seem, is itself extended significantly by vesting it in the king.

But it is not merely a matter of lodging discretionary power with the king. For the use of discretionary power is now not an incidental activity but a significant element in the profile of both monarchy and the courts and, even more, a major component of their role in society. Maimonides makes this statement by the artful use of literary devices, of which he is a master, as well as by substantive rulings. He does not merely enable king and court to use discretionary power, he instructs them to do so, stating his rulings in the imperative. The phraseology repeats the value-saturated terms used to describe the basic goals of government, phrases such as "breaking the arms of the wicked," or, more generally, "the mending of society."[21] With respect to the court, Maimonides assembles rulings dealing with all the various modes of discretionary power, ranging from the court's obligation to decide civil cases on the basis of its own perceptions, despite testimony to the contrary, to its obligation to impose punishments of extraordinary severity even when normal standards of evidence are not met, to its obligation to impose *herem* and *niddui*, to expropriate property as a punitive device, and finally to engage in prophetic rebuke and chastisement. We shall have occasion to return in more detail to certain aspects of the twenty-four chapters of *Hilchot Sanedrin*; suffice it to say that in this chapter, varied as its elements may be, Maimonides is intent on one overriding goal: the creation of the court as an organ capable of using discretionary powers frequently and powerfully. Maimonides thus suggests that neither the civil nor the religious order of society can survive if defended by the more delicate normative structures alone. It is well worth noting, parenthetically, that Maimonides seems to have an abiding interest in the general issue of temporary, extraordinary suspension of permanent, standard norms; for he explores this topic not only in connection with the court's role vis-à-vis society but also vis-à-vis the legal structure itself, insofar as both court and prophet may (and are expected to) temporarily suspend laws of the Torah and instruct the populace to violate its sacred norms, if judged necessary.[22]

One topic is especially singled out as warranting application of standards beyond those of the normal normative order—murder. Generally speaking, Maimonides views murder as especially worthy of punishment for, "although there are sins worse than bloodshed, none cause the destruction of civilized society as does bloodshed. Not even idolatry, nor sexual immorality, nor desecration of the Sabbath, is the equal of bloodshed."[23] Thus, there exists a whole range of situations in which the court must judge the murderer innocent by its normal procedures but is also expected to punish him severely, in the interests of social order by applying another, much more functional standard of judgment. Here are two examples. Maimonides rules that the king ought to disregard the normal rule requiring two witnesses to the act and full acknowledgment by the would-be murderer of a warning before the act, in order to convict.[24] The rigorous and ideal norms obviously make it virtually impossible to convict any criminal. Second, while the fully normative structures do not convict for conspiracy or any act other than the physical and direct act of murder, Maimonides rules that both king and court may execute in such cases (again, "for the benefit of society" in the case of the king, and "provided that circumstances warrant such action" for the court), and must "flog, . . . imprison, . . . and inflict severe punishment . . . in order to frighten and terrify other wicked persons, lest such a case become a pitfall and a snare."[25] Islamic jurisprudence, confronted by similarly rigorous norms (in the laws of evidence, for example), also declared that its *mazalim* courts must act for the benefit of society and apply a more realistic standard of justice.[26]

Maimonides thought, then, that society could be maintained only by granting the organs of governance sweeping discretionary powers, which he expected would be used frequently, or at least would be a very visible deterrent. At the same time, it is difficult to discover any systematic categorization underlying this state of affairs. Maimonides does not speak of two bodies of law, each appropriate to different types of society or to different aspects of the same society. Indeed, since he is a legist rather than a philosopher of law (in our context, of course), it may be unfair to expect him to produce such a conceptualization. Nor is the distinction between discretionary power and normative law institutionalized in the sense that different persons and bodies are responsible for each. Both king and court wield discretionary powers; and if this seems confusing, it is merely part of the much larger problematic of separating the functions of king and court in Judaic political theory from biblical times.[27] Maimonides does not distinguish, then, between "ideal" and "real." He does distinguish, explicitly and repeatedly, between instances where only individuals are affected and in which rigorous normative law is to be applied, and situations of great social resonance where the public good is involved and in which government must exercise its prerogative and set aside the norms that are usually operative.[28]

However effective all this may turn out to be, it is obvious that it also opens the door to despotism and tyranny. Prerogative power, writes John Dunn, "eludes that careful tissue of legal restraint which men have devised over the centuries for their protection against their rulers";[29] and even if this modern comment on Locke is probably not fully acceptable to a medieval Jew like Maimonides, it is clear that he too was aware of the abuses to which discretionary power lent itself. Thus, the major statement on the discretionary power of the court concludes with a warning that judges should remain sensitive to the human dignity of those they punish, and continues to rail against undue assertion by communal leaders.[30] Yet all these admonitions do not fully solve the problem; they possess no sanction and their relevance is left totally to the evaluation and conscience of the judge or communal leader himself.

It is significant, therefore, that Maimonides's recommendation of discretionary power is not quite as radically unregulated and unchecked as one might assume from a superficial reading.

Maimonides clearly prefers to endow the court, rather than the king, with the prerogative of overriding normative law. He does extend this power to the king as well, but, it would appear, in cases of bloodshed alone. In all other situations where discretionary power is allowed, he speaks—as does the Talmud—of the court. It is likely that Maimonides was wary of adding to the power already granted the king and that he hoped that the men who in general administered the law—judges— would not easily undermine it. From a more systematic point of view, the ability of the court (rather than the king) to absorb this major social function reflects the division of powers basic to Jewish political theory, which places all judicial responsibility in the hands of an independent judiciary.[31]

Moreover, the power to deal with extraordinary situations is not delegated to a judicial arm specially created for that purpose, a body of courts distinct from the normal framework of the judicial system and independent of its standards. This, of course, is the case with the Islamic *mazalim*, whose appointment by the *khalif* reflects the centralized structure of the Islamic polity.[32] In the halakhic regime, discretionary power is to be integrated into the workings of the general court system (much as it is integrated by Maimonides, from a literary point of view, into his *Code*); it is viewed as an integral and fully legitimate aspect of Jewish law, requiring neither apology, subterfuge, nor a guilty conscience.[33] Maimonides does allow the king to appoint judges, parallel to the appointment of judges by the judiciary itself.[34] But while this procedure remains only too vague in both details and overall conception, certain points are clear: the king may appoint only fully qualified men to serve as judges; and, more significantly, there is no reason to think that these apply a law any different from that of the court-appointed judges, or that they are to constitute an independent system based on powers of prerogative. Maimonides's determination to keep the use of prerogative powers on a short leash, as it were, also influenced his development of the institution of the market-inspector. The Maimonidean *shoter* is, most probably, heavily indebted to the Islamic *muhtasib* in the range of his responsibilities; but Maimonides makes it clear that the *shoter* is a court-appointed official and he is quite reluctant to grant this official the power of summary punishment with which the *muhtasib* is endowed.[35]

These restraints on the actual use of discretionary powers ought to be supplemented by a number of more theoretical considerations, the broad thrust of which is to argue that even discretionary power must be defined by both law and morality, or, put another way, that Maimonides felt that the license to abandon the more rigorous normative structures did not necessarily impair the law's quest for truth or justice. Let us take as an example the overall relaxation of the normal rules of evidence. In cases guided by the public good, the courts or king may punish, as we have seen, with less than the two witnesses mandated by biblical law, and even without the normal warning and acknowledgment by the accused. Actually, it is likely that *two* witnesses are not required—but that *one* is.[36] This, though, is not the heart of my point. Simply put, it is that Maimonides often indicates that one witness may lead a court to the truth no less than two, and that this requirement, along with that of warning and acknowledgment, may well be of a formal and even dogmatic nature. Thus, he will speak of cases in which "the testimony of the witnesses could not be sustained for some reason, preventing application of the penalty, such as the lack of prior warning or a contradiction in minor details—though it [the testimony] is true," and the criminal ought to be punished.[37] It is assumed in a

number of contexts that these aspects of the law of evidence are basi-
cally formal and are not necessary for ascertaining the truth. One such
indication—which bears other implications as well for our subject—is
Maimonides's firm declaration that the fundamental and original basis
of civil-law decisions is that "the judge should act in accordance with
what he is inclined to believe is the truth when he feels strongly that
his belief is justified, though he has no actual proof of it," and that the
current practice of deciding on the basis of "clear evidence" only is the
necessary result of a decline in both moral and intellectual levels.[38]
Significantly, this discussion heads the twenty-fourth chapter in *Laws
of the Sanhedrin* and is doubtless intended to give this chapter (in
which discretionary power is laid out) its moral basis within the overall
structures of Jewish law. And, if I may briefly tick off some other
instances (among which are cases in criminal law): criminals can be
disqualified as unfit witnesses, even if they acted without warning and
acknowledgment, if it can be assumed that they knew the seriousness
of their act;[39] a blood-avenger may act on the basis of testimony of a
single witness;[40] a criminal may be imprisoned (*kipah*) even if the
formal requirements are not met.[41]

All this means that Maimonides conceives of discretionary power as
occupying a different level of the Jewish legal structure, but not as
operating outside this structure *in toto*. Certain basic safeguards must
be retained. And, not infrequently, discretionary power is used to out-
flank a legal formalism (or ideal) that endangers the public good.
Maimonides does not seem to conceive of a discretionary power that
sacrifices the totally innocent in the interests of the common good.

A second, more theoretical, consideration supports this analysis. It
has been shown (and this was already known in the fourteenth century)
that the basic pattern of discretionary power within the Jewish commonwealth is virtually identical with the normal functioning of the
Noahide legal system that was expected to govern humankind as a
whole. To be more precise, this is the pattern of discretionary power as
Maimonides created it. Many of the norms mentioned earlier, such as
the duty to punish conspirators or indirect actors and the possibility of
punishment without warning or acknowledgment, are found only in the
Talmudic discussion of Noahide law; it is Maimonides who carries
them over to Jewish discretionary law. Indeed, it is quite likely that
Maimonides's entire edifice of monarchic powers identifies Jewish and
gentile governance as a single structure possessing similiar goals and

utilizing similar instruments.[42] Obviously, the idea that Jewish society is regulated by both Noahide and Judaic law may suggest some sort of "two-tier" theory, and we shall soon see how this becomes explicit in a fourteenth-century interpretation of Maimonides. (Parenthetically, we ought to recall that, through Maimonides, the concept of Noahide law became a major source for Grotius's discussion of international natural law.) In our present discussion of whether discretionary power is bounded by some limiting mechanism, we ought to stress that the identification of discretionary power with Noahide law means that it reflects a normative structure, that it is morally legitimated, and that it is limited by this very structure. When Maimonides introduces the topic by assuring us, for example, that conspirators to murder are in fact murderers and will be punished by God, he provides the moral basis for a human court's taking the matter into its own hands.[43] Without this basis, he suggests, neither Noahide law nor discretionary power would be free to act. Public safety is not an absolute criterion. Even if king and court are free to set aside both procedural and substantive rules of law when the good—either physical or spiritual—of society warrants it, they must remain within the broad consensus of moral values constituting society.

One further consideration ought to be kept in mind when we discuss the mechanisms limiting the use of discretionary power. Maimonides, it is most likely, thought that a king could be deposed (probably by the High Court, the Great Sanhedrin) for objective reasons.[44] It is fair to extrapolate, then, that while the king was charged with acting for the public good and was expected to exercise his prerogative power to that purpose, his activity was also subject to the scrutiny of the court. This scrutiny, and the sanction it could deliver, represent a constitutional control of abuse of prerogative power by the king. Of course, this provides no solution to the abuse of this power by the court itself; and, as we have seen, the court's power of prerogative is more extensive than that of the king.

Nissim

> This leads to the following situations: first, that a criminal can be punished according to the dictates of true justice [*mishpat amiti*]; and second, that even when no punishment is deserved according to true justice, he will be punished for the good of the public order and the

need of the hour. Now the Lord distinguished between those responsible for each of these two tasks: The courts are to decide according to the
true and just law ... And since the political order cannot be perfected
by this alone, the Lord commmanded kingship so as to achieve this
perfection.[45]

This is Rabbi Nissim of Gerona (Ran), a fourteenth-century legist and
thinker, in his Eleventh Homily. Here the ideas with which we are
familiar are now explicitly proclaimed to be the ideological infrastructure of the legal and political structures. Here we find explicit conceptualization, firm systematization, and concrete institutionalization. It is
all neatly packaged, with nary a loose end in the ribbon: two modes of
social control, representing two distinct goals, and delegated to two
distinct institutions. Ideal justice is to govern the relationship between
individuals so long as it does not damage the rather coarser bonds of
society; and a different type of rule, that of political justice, is to
govern when social cohesion and public order must be guaranteed.

Let us summarize this doctrine in more detail, and then suggest *its*
ideological underpinnings. We have already noted the essential distinction between true justice and what is required for the good of society.
It would be helpful were Rabbi Nissim to have defined the *limits*; that
is, to what lengths does society go in denying "true justice" so as to
assure its safety and order, a point about which Maimonides may,
perhaps, have been sensitive. But let us recall that Rabbi Nissim is
writing a sermon, not recording legal regulations. This fact goes far to
explain, of course, why he found it necessary to conceptualize our
topic to begin with, and to argue the legitimacy of the arrangements he
discerned in the legal materials. Yet it is interesting that the issue of
limits, as well as the question of the relationship between the two
institutions of court and king, were not at the heart of his concern,
which was, apparently, to produce a defense of the apparent duality
and provide a Jewish model of political power. The two institutions are
firmly distinguished and little overlap is allowed. This systematization
goes far beyond what we have seen until now, where courts handle
discretionary power no less, and indeed more, than do kings. Indeed,
Rabbi Nissim is so committed to this conceptualization that he is
forced to argue that "monarchy" is not a matter of personal identity but
rather a power, and that this power is lodged in the courts when no
king sits on the throne.[46] (Actually, this having it both ways is not

uncommon in discussions of our topic.) Finally, Rabbi Nissim argues that monarchy is an institution common to both gentiles and the people of Israel, for all must create a stable political order. The ideal and practice of true justice, though, is a uniquely Jewish task for which no model exists in the gentile world. (This, if meant in more than the abstract mode, is a rather nasty swipe at the society in which the author lived.)

What are the Jewish sources of this rather elegant, if highly dualistic and schematized, model? Certainly, there is a very heavy Maimonidean input, especially as regards the concrete halakhic materials found in the Homily: in the need for strong governance and in the assumption that the usual normative structures are not fully adequate to this need, and hence in the overall weight attached to the use of discretionary powers; in the significance of the monarchy and its possession of discretionary powers; in the identification of Jewish and gentile modes of governance so far as social control is concerned. Rabbi Nissim undoubtedly and correctly saw himself as an interpreter of Maimonides, perhaps as one who provided the explicit conceptualization that Maimonides, as legist, had left beneath the surface. Yet it seems to me that Maimonides is less dualistic, on the whole, than is Rabbi Nissim. He does not see the rigorously normative ideal, justice, over against which is reared the edifice of social justice. Nor does he project the sharp contrast of king and court that is central to Ran's description. There is much more mesh and overlap, and this can be seen in the fact that, in Maimonides, the court is a basic exponent of both norms and prerogative. Perhaps, too, this is the reason that Maimonides shows sensitivity to the issue of limits, an issue that Rabbi Nissim sees as too peripheral for discussion. For these and other reasons, I think that we must dig elsewhere to lay bare Nissim's intellectual roots—in the direction of Judah Ha-Levi (1085–1140).

The significance of Ha-Levi is first felt on the literary and linguistic levels. At the very start of his Homily, Rabbi Nissim approvingly cites the view that "even a band of robbers must abide by a standard of honesty"—virtually a verbatim quote of *Kuzari* 2:48.[47] And Ha-Levi goes on to develop the notion (which differs somewhat from his own discussion of the law appropriate to philosophers in 1:13, or the Maimonidean notions discussed earlier) of a social-ethical law appropriate to gentiles to which is then added the spiritual-ceremonial law given to Israel. More significant, though, is Rabbi Nissim's description of the divine commands of religion as designed to "bring the divine overflow upon our people and to cleave to us, . . . which is achieved by actions though they be far from rational understanding."[48] This is Ha-Levi's language, not Maimonides's. Most significant is the application of this characterization to the social norms contained in the Torah:

> And so I think that just as the religious commands [hukkim] have no social function but are the cause of bringing upon us the divine over-flow, so too the civil and criminal law [mishpatim] of the Torah is a cause of both our people's receiving the divine overflow and of its social order. And it is possible that this body of law is really directed to the higher goal rather than to the goal of social order, for that is achieved by the king whom we appoint.[49]

The norms of the Torah, then, are not merely ideal. "True justice" is defined as law that has no social function. This attempt to describe as much of the Torah as possible as being inaccessible to human needs, and in that sense to practical reason,[50] is, of course, characteristic of Ha-Levi. We ought also to recall that the monarchy or its equivalent occupies a rather insignificant place in Ha-Levi's understanding of the structure of leadership and authority in the people Israel, as the people of God.[51]

Rabbi Nissim describes the normative structures of Jewish law as highly ideal and for that reason unable to control social reality. Consequently, he also disengages the institutional embodiment of the ideal law, the court, from society. The great vacuum that is thus created can be filled only by a monarchy that is liberated from the restrictive norms of the Torah. Paradoxically, the assertion that the Torah represents "true justice" and nothing less forces it to relinquish its social role and to deliver the task of governing society to a monarch whose power, it would seem, is limited only by his conscience.

Indeed, whatever advantages this arrangement may have held, Rabbi Nissim is also aware of its dangers. And so, despite his assertion that the monarchy is commanded by God so that the Jewish people, like all other peoples, will be governed more efficiently than a regime of "true justice" would allow, Rabbi Nissim pulls back. The people sinned by asking a king of Samuel, he agrees; they wished to be ruled by a king's political justice, rather than by the "true justice" of the Torah and its courts, which would have brought "the divine influence" to rest upon them.[52] And then he adds that the limits set by the Bible on the king's wealth, and the command that the king write a Torah scroll for himself, are attempts to control the monarch, "for since the king sees that he is not as subject to the laws of the Torah as is the judge, he requires greater warning lest he stray from the Law and lest he rise up arrogantly above his brethren, because of the great power which the Lord has given him."[53] Rabbi Nissim doubtless realized that these traces would be easily snapped by a headstrong monarch, as Talmudic law had in fact been forced to concede; and moreover, that the normative structure itself might not even provide a full remedy. And so toward the end of the Eleventh Homily, Rabbi Nissim gives another reason why the king ought not to lord it over his people. For, he says, citing Rabbi Jonah of Gerona (d. 1263), "the king rules in proportion to the honor and recognition given by the masses, so that if they deprive him of all that honor, they will also be completely free of their king."[54] Or, to speak in terms of the overall structure, even the vast powers given the state are in the service of the people and the prudent ruler will always remember that.

What can we say about the historical backgrounds of this picture? Two contemporary perspectives ought to be suggested—that of the general, gentile, society within which Rabbi Nissim's Jewish reality existed, and that of the Jewish community itself.

Rabbi Nissim did not live in Muslim Spain, where the contrast of "ideal" and "real" states and their corresponding political correlates was a commonplace. Christian Spain knew, of course, the doctrine of the Two Cities, but that is quite a different matter. Yet Ran's sharp distinction between king and court—a distinction alien to the highly centralized Islamic political thought and, as we have seen, much sharper than that drawn in Maimonides—is not terribly remote from the Gelasian apposition of king and pope.[55] On the political level, Rabbi Nissim's portrayal of the king ought to be read, perhaps, in the light of certain thirteenth–fourteenth century developments. The Civilians Bartolus and Baldus speak for a position according to which "the supreme and absolute authority of the prince is not under the law"; and we may also recall the violent conflicts of Boniface VII and Philip the Fair, which were formulated, in part, in terms of the power of the king to violate laws in cases of absolute necessity or the good of the state.[56] On the other hand, it is unlikely that Rabbi Nissim was unaware of the thirteenth-century Unionist conflict in Aragon, which issued in the

Privilegio General of 1287 with its deposition clause, a conflict that flared up again in 1347–49.[57] These circumstances give added bite to Rabbi Jonah Gerondi's comment cited above, as well as to Ran's general discussion of the election of kings.

And what of the perspective provided by Jewish political history? Rabbi Nissim is clearly intent on delivering power to its legitimate wielders, even power to overrule the laws of the Torah for the good of his society. Taken broadly, Rabbi Nissim offers religious reassurance to the Spanish Jewish communities, agreeing that they could not assert effective social control if they abided by the stringent norms of Talmudic law. Rabbi Solomon ibn Adret, an older contemporary of Ran, had said much the same thing in more pithy fashion; and Rabbi Asher ben Yehiel also noted that the practices of Spanish Jewry were necessarily more remote from Talmudic law than those of his Ashkenazic brethren. Indeed, the doctrines of ibn Adret contribute to the whole picture. As pointed out by Daniel Gutenmacher,[58] Rashba had applied the Talmudic doctrine of Sanhedrin 46a, the doctrine of discretionary power, in two related ways: (a) he applied it to the community rather than restricting it to the court, and thus duplicated a step taken by Ashkenazic legists some centuries earlier; and (b) he approved of discretionary power not only as a mode of meeting specific, irregular forms of behavior that posed social dangers, but rather as the rule of government itself, as an ongoing activity maintained by the community. Thus Rashba speaks not only of the *judicial* responsibility of the community but also of its *legislative* and *administrative* tasks. These positions, I would argue, dovetail with the concern underlying Rabbi Nissim's writing, a concern that the community be endowed with the power necessary for self-preservation. This reading stresses Ran's constitutional acknowledgment of legal pragmatism, rather than the institutional differentiation to which he devotes much attention. But perhaps we ought to suggest a narrower but more specific reading, according to which Rabbi Nissim is an interested party delivering power to the courts, which were of course manned by his own fraternity, the clerical scholar class. I do not see too much evidence for this position. There is little in the sermon that even hints at the institutional conflicts in the Spanish Jewish community. It is far from clear that "monarchy" and "court" served as rigorous metaphors for loci of political power in the contemporary community; if the language of ibn Adret is an indicator, each served equally well in a more diffuse political tradition.[59] Rabbi Nissim, morover, goes so far as to suggest (in the passage given in note 52) that the court (!) is never endowed with the same broad prerogative in civil or criminal law as it is in the purely religious sphere—hardly the kind of admission an advocate of clerical power ought to make. Here, in fact, the moribund "monarchy" would have to be revived and identified as the community itself for Ran's doctrine to have any practical effect!

Be all this as it may, Rabbi Nissim has developed the distinction between the "real" and the "ideal" about as far as it will go in Jewish political theory. Curiously, his work is a focus of attention in today's Israel, as it offers religous legitimacy to a state that orders its society by norms that do not always dovetail with classic Jewish law.[60] Yet, we may feel uneasy about the potential of this doctrine, which can so easily be used to justify virtually any abuse of centralized power; and Rabbi Nissim was aware of this sinister potential. Detachment of the "real" from the "ideal" is a dangerous step; we almost sense Machiavelli waiting in the wings. In that sense, the fifteenth-century anti-monarchic critique of Abrabanel, a critique that includes Rabbi Nissim among its targets, is a natural and indeed expected continuation of the trajectory we have studied.

Conclusion

It is a presupposition of Jewish social life that this society will be self-governing. This assumption is one of the bases of Jewish communal life in premodern times, and it most likely informed the Jew's consciousness as an individual relating to his fellows. Self-government dovetailed, as Robert Chazan tells us in this volume, with the structures of pre-modern political relationships with national minorities, to be sure. And self-government is mandated, last but not least, by Jewish law. The Torah, of course, envisions not only a self-subsisting people, but one that eagerly embraces many of the functions of governance, even as it rushes, perhaps foolhardily, into certain institutional arrangements (e.g., kingship). The subsequent history of Jewish law in exile and diaspora apparently remains loyal to this founding vision.

Jewish law and teaching provided its people, then, with a standard of behavior encompassing life's varied agenda, ranging from the experiences of the individual *qua* individual to his performances as a member of the collective. And along with these standards, it also provided a regimen of institutions and sanctions designed to enforce them.

But it would seem that the sanctions and procedural elements of Jewish law, its political function, has had an essentially different career than other normative elements of Judaism. While Jewish law (in both its sacred and civil aspects) has, in general, pursued a path consonant with its own immanent thrust as well as with the pressures of historical reality, this has not been the case as regards the political norms. Here, rather, we can sense the presence of a significant body of discretionary powers and extraordinary remedies, leading to what has been called (in the Islamic sphere) the "two-tier" theory of law. Briefly put, this theory maintains that the law as specified in the codes and legal literature applies only to an ideal society; the managing of historical reality, which departs from the ideal, demands the disavowal of these norms and the arming of those responsible for public safety and order with broad discretionary power.

The Talmud is, in all truth, quite reticent on this issue. It does report the use of extraordinary, discretionary remedies, and expressly legitimates them for times of emergency. But these do not seem to play a generative role, nor does the Talmud suggest any overarching theory that would integrate the "ideal" and "real." This phenomenon is greatly enlarged in the legal writings of Maimonides, who assigns these powers a significant role in the governance of society. Maimonides does seem to imply the need to impose some limits on this doctrine, but all in all his willingness to empower both king and court with discretionary powers reflects his basic quest for social stability. These Maimonidean positions are the springboard for an explicit "two-tier" theory in the work of the fourteenth-century Rabbi Nissim, who also argues for an institutional embodiment of the dichotomy, with the monarchy becoming the locus of the "real," and the Great Court that of the "ideal." While ostensibly Maimonidean, the deeper roots of this conceptualization lie equally in the thought of Judah Ha-Levi.

Rabbi Nissim was subsequently attacked for the concessions his theory made to reality at the expense of the revealed law of the Torah. In a sense, his doctrine reflects the political realities of his time—Christian political theory as well as the actual political practice of the Jewish community. At the same time it is, of course, an attempt to conceptualize aspects of Jewish law and governance. Modern Israeli religionists who seek halakhic legitimation of nonhalakhic legislation have obviously found a historic ally in Rabbi Nissim. In the Islamic

sphere, we recall, this phenomenon has ostensibly led to broad demoralization, and one wonders whether (if that analysis is in fact accurate)
a similar pattern is noticeable in Jewish life; and if, as seems to be the
case, it is not—then why not?[61]

Notes

1. *Responsa Rashba*, 3:393; cited by R. Joseph Karo, *Beit Yosef* to *Tur,
Hoshen Mishpat*, 2.
2. I have found the following, all dealing with Islamic political and legal
theory, suggestive for the Jewish problematic as well: H. Gibb, "Constitutional
Organization," in M. Khadduri, *Law in the Middle East*, I (Washington, DC: The
Middle East Institute, 1955), pp. 3–28; R. Maydani, "Uqubat: Penal Law," in
ibid., pp. 223–35; E. Tynan, "Judicial Organization," in ibid., pp. 235–78; M.H.
Kerr, *Islamic Reform* (Berkeley: University of California Press, 1966); N.J. Coulson, *Conflicts and Tensions in Islamic Jurisprudence* (Chicago: University of
Chicago Press, 1969). See also the materials cited below in notes 3, 24, and
30. Kerr has suggested that, as a religious system, Islam remains vague and
nonspecific on basic constitutional issues; it would be interesting to pursue this
question in the Jewish context as well.
3. See D. Pipes, *In the Path of God: Islam and Political Power* (New York:
Basic Books, 1983), pp. 41–63, and bibliographic references.
4. The rabbis will even claim that some provisions of *biblical* law depart from
the ideal and are concessions to human weakness: see b. *Kiddushin* 21a (the
captive woman) and b. *Sanhedrin* 20b (the monarchy).
5. *Tosefta Sanhedrin* 4:2 (ed. Zukermandel, p. 420).
6. *M. Sanhedrin* 2:2 and b. *Sanhedrin* 19a–b; the different construction found
in the Palestinian Talmud ad loc. is not our concern here. For a "constitutional"
understanding of this Mishnaic provision, see P. Dickstein, "Mishpat uMedina
BeYisrael," *HaTekufah* 28 (1936), pp. 363–74.
7. See, for example, *M. Sotah* 9:9 and b. *Avodah Zarah* 8b: "When murderers
became many the rite of breaking the heifer's neck ceased ... when adulterers
became many the rite of the bitter waters ceased"; "Said R. Nahman b. Isaac, ...
when the Sanhedrin say that murderers were so prevalent that they could not be
properly dealt with judicially, they said: 'Rather let us be exiled from place to
place. . . .' "
8. b. *Sanhedrin* 46a; p. *Hagigah* 2:2 (78a); and see below, note 26. We are
interested, of course, in the Talmud perception and understanding of these events;
the question of whether the "extraordinary" penalties imposed were in fact normative in earlier historical periods is not our concern. For textual comparison of the
Babylonian and Palestinian versions, see M. Elon, *Hamishpat HaIvri*, II (Jerusalem: Magnes, 1973), p. 422, n. 94. For a general discussion of the overall issue,
see H. Ben-Menachem, "Setiyyat HaShofet Min Hadin," *Shenaton Hamishpat
HaIvri*, 8 (1981): 113–34.
9. p. Hagigah, 2:2 (78a), where the discussion is amoraic. See Ben-
Menachem, "Setiyyat HaShofet Min Hadin," pp. 126–27.

10. See b. *Ketubot* 27b and Rashi; b. *Baba Kamma* 96b and Rif; b. *Sanhedrin* 27a–b and Rashi (here an *amorah* is acting in the service [?] of the *resh galuta*); b. *Baba Kamma* 116b–117a and Rashi.

11. It ought to be noted that the examples provided by the *baraitha* all concern religious law or morals, and not civil or criminal law. This was pointed out by Rabbi Ephraim, a twelfth-century student of Rabbi Alfas, in apparent objection to his master's extended use of the doctrine (*Temim De'im*, 68; to Rif at *B.K.* 96b); it is also at the heart of Ran's comment, cited in note 45, whose context is a discussion of the *Sanhedrin* 46a passage. See also note 15.

12. Further discretionary powers are given in b. *Mo'ed Katan* 16a. "[W]e may quarrel [with the offender], curse him, smite him, pluck his hair out, bind him, imprison him"; these are derived from *Nehemiah* 13:25 and *Ezra* 7:26. I consider these powers discretionary because the Talmud does not specify in which circumstances they are to be used, nor is it clear that the list is exhaustive. It is noteworthy (a) that the Talmud does not relate to the power to execute, listed in Ezra 7; (b) that these powers are derived from an edict of a gentile king, Artaxerxes; and (c) that the Palestinian Talmud does not, apparently, know of these powers. Another similar pattern describes the penalties imposed on informers and the like: *Tosefta Baba Mezi'ah* 2:33 (ed. Zukermandel, p. 375).

13. See I. Herzog, *The Main Institutions of Jewish Law* (London: Soncino, 1936), I, pp. 55–56. Recent research indicates that this broad generalization needs considerable qualification. See for example S. Rosenberg's seminal essay, "VeShuv Al Derakh HaRov," in E. Belfer, ed., *Manhigut Ruhanit BeYisrael* (Tel Aviv: Dvir, 1982), pp. 87–102.

14. This is stressed in certain medieval collections (see note 38) on the basis of Talmudic materials, both Babylonian and Palestinian (see b. *Ketubot* 85b and p. *Baba Kamma* 10:1).

15. b. *Sanhedrin* 32a–b; p. *Sanhedrin* 4:1 (22a).

16. b. *Sanhedrin* 2b–3a. Some of these problems were often solved in more artificial but less disruptive ways; see b. *Gittin* 88b, b. *Baba Kamma* 84a–b, etc. Yet despite all this activity, further legal measures had to be devised in the geonic period to allow collection of fines and other payments that were constitutionally unactionable outside the land of Israel; the materials are collected in A. Aptowitzer, *Mehkarim* (Jerusalem: Mosad HaRav Kook, 1941) pp. 97–122.

17. I do not intend to suggest that Maimonides was the first to read, say, the *baraitha* b. *Sanhedrin* 46a expansively. This tendency is already found in Rabbi Alfas (note 10) and his student Rabbi Joseph ibn Megas (*Responsa*, 161), and it is reflected in the commentary of Rashi (note 11). The *baraitha* also forms part of the preamble of the text of local enactments as recorded by Rabbi Judah al-Barceloni, *Sefer HaShetarot* (Berlin: Izkovski, 1898), p. 134. I do not recall seeing geonic exploitation of this *baraitha*. See, in general, S. Albeck, "Yesodot Mishtar HaKehillot," *Zion*, 25 (1960): 106–14. This Maimonidean tendency has been noted by H. Cohen, "Maimonides' Theory of Codification," *Jewish Law Annual* I (1978), p. 34; and see now D. Biale, *Power and Powerlessness in Jewish History* (New York: Schocken, 1986), pp. 51–53.

18. *H. Rozeah* 2:1–5; *H. Melakhim* 3:10.

19. See the incident involving the Exilarch (*resh galut*), whom Maimonides assimilates to a monarchic figure (*H. Sanhedrin* 4:13). See also b. *Sanhedrin* 5a

and parallels. The Talmud is also wary of monarchic desires to disregard the norms of legal procedure; see b. *Rosh HaShannah* 21b.

20. *H. Sanhedrin* 4:13–14 (the expansion of b. *Sanhedrin* 5a to imply the authority to appoint judges as well as the right to free them from payment of damages is explicit in geonic literature and reflects historical reality); ibid. 3:8.

21. Compare *H. Melakhim* 3:10 and 4:10.

22. *H. Yesodai HaTorah* 9:3–5; *H. Mamrim* 2:4. In recapitulating our *baraitha*, *H. Sanhedrin* 24:4, Maimonides also adds the cautionary phrase, *hora' at sha'ah*.

23. *H. Rozeah* 4:9. I have used with slight adaption the translation of H. Klein, *The Code of Maimonides: The Book of Torts* (New Haven: Yale University Press, 1954), p. 207.

24. *H. Melakhim* 3:10. It is, of course, suggestive to speculate as to whether the institution of *hatra' ah* had reached full development before the Jewish judiciary stopped functioning normally—that is, during the Second Temple period—or whether it is in large part the product of legal theorists. See Z. Falk, *Introduction to Jewish Law of the Second Commonwealth*, I (Leiden: E.J. Brill, 1972), pp. 119–21. That the Pharisees were loath to impose severe penalties is well known, as are the rabbinic tendencies to minimize use of the death penalty.

25. *H. Rozeah* 2:4–5. Another instance where Maimonides distinguishes between the steps to be taken in cases in which an individual is harmed and those appropriate to a broad social threat concerns recourse to gentile authority: "if one oppresses the community, ... it is permissible to hand him over to the gentile authorities to be beaten, imprisoned, and fined. But if one merely distresses an individual, he must not be handed over" (*H. Hovel uMazik* 8:11).

26. See Tynan, "Judicial Organization," pp. 236, 263–69; N. Coulson, *A History of Islamic Law* (Edinburgh: University of Edinburgh Press, 1964), pp. 132–44. See also S. Baron, *Social and Religious History of the Jewish People* (Philadephia: Jewish Publication Society, 1957), p. 20, on the parallelism of the prerogative of the judge in Jewish law, and the Islamic institution of *ta azir*.

27. See R. de Vaux, *Ancient Israel* (New York: McGraw-Hill, 1951), pp. 150–54; Z. Frankel, *Der gerichtliche Beweise* (Berlin, 1846), pp. 40 ff. For a fuller discussion, see Y. Blidstein, *Ekronot Mediniyyim BeMishnat HaRambam* (Ramat-Gan: Bar-Ilan University Press, 1983), pp. 92–93, 119–47.

28. In this, of course, he picks up the Talmudic cautionary note. But he also expands: The Talmud does not limit Ezra 7:26 (see note 12) to extraordinary situations, but that is how Maimonides incorporates it in his Code (*H. Sanhedrin* 24:8–10).

29. J. Dunn, *The Political Thought of John Locke* (Cambridge: Cambridge University Press, 1969), pp. 148–56. (My thanks to my colleague Dr. Haim Marantz, who pointed me in the direction of Dunn.) Locke had allowed the sovereign a prerogative power, which is "the people's permitting the rulers to do ... things ... sometimes against the direct letter of the law for the public good" (*Two Treatises on Civil Government*, sec. 164). This doctrine was rejected both in England and the United States; see E. Fraenkel, *The Dual State* (New York: Oxford University Press, 1941), pp. 66–69. The modern bureaucratic state, it has been pointed out, is rife with prerogative.

30. *H. Sanhedrin* 24:10–25;2.

31. See S. Cohen, "The Concept of the Three Ketarim: Its Place in Jewish

Political Thought," *AJS Review*, 9, no. 1 (Spring 1984): 27–54.

32. "Islamic political theory is not based upon the principle of the separation of powers. Supreme executive and judicial power is vested in the sovereign, and by the process of delegation each and every official of the State becomes his representative. Judicial competence results only from appointment by the ruler; the jurists admit the right of the ruler to restrict the competence of the *qadi* by forbidding him to hear certain cases or types of cases; and further they recognize that in the majority of instances the *qadi* is entirely dependent upon the political authority for the execution of his judgments. . . . Since . . . it was perfectly legitimate for the ruler to delegate full or limited judicial competence to officials of the State other than the *qadi*, the jurists were forced to recognize the so-called extra-Shari'ah tribunals. . . . For in the event the powers and functions of the executive authorities will depend upon the discretion of the ruler." N. Coulson, "The State and the Individual in Islamic Law," *International and Comparative Law Quarterly*, 6 (1957). See also note 26.

33. Structurally, this is the judicial parallel to the rabbinic power of *takkanah* vis-à-vis the law itself: *takkanah*, too, is considered part and parcel of the Oral Law in the broad sense of the term. Such internalization may prevent the demoralization of which researchers of Islam speak (Pipes, *In the Path of God*), though I am not fully convinced by their description in any case.

34. *H. Rozeah* 2:1–5; *H. Melakhim* 3:10.

35. See *H. Genevah* 8:20; *H. Sanhedrin* 1:2: *Sefer HaMitzvot*, Aseh 176. The presence of *muhtasib* in the Maimonidean *shoter* was first noted by S. Baron, "Economic Views of Maimonides," in S. Baron, ed., *Essays on Maimonides* (New York: Columbia University Press, 1941), p. 173, n. 93. My discussion of the authority of the *shoter* has appeared (in Hebrew) in *Shenaton HaMishpat HaIvri*, 14–15 (1988–89): 89–94.

36. See *H. Melakhim* 3:10, and in general Blidstein, *Ekronot Mediniyyim BeMishnat HaRambam*, pp. 123–26. But see Guide 3:40, according to which the monarch may punish "on presumption," although a single—if unfit—witness is mentioned.

37. *Perush HaMishnah, Sanhedrin* 9:5.

38. *H. Sanhedrin* 24:1–3. This is an excellent instance of Maimonides shaping a Talmudic source (b. *Ketubot* 85b) and enlarging upon it in terms of a broader position: compare the treatment of Rabbi Alfas ad loc! Note paragraph 3, where Maimonides points out that even in present times, a judge is not to accept testimony that runs counter to his intuitions as probative. For the general Talmudic basis of these Maimonidean positions, see H. Hefez, "Dinei Umdenah," *Dinei Yisra'el* 8 (1977): 45–64; idem, "Mekomah Shel Edut," *Dinei Yisra'el* 9 (1978–1980): 51–84. Other instances of Maimonidean insistence that the court use its good judgment are *H. Malveh VeLoveh* 2:4 (and note the proviso as to the court's motivation), and 23:2; *H. She'elah U-Pikadon* 6:4. For a most interesting instance of Maimonides's own utilization of these rules, see *Responsa* (ed. J. Blau), no. 365, pp. 640–41, as compared with *H. Ishut* 13:19–20.

39. *H. Edut* 12:1.

40. *H. Rozeah* 6:5, and note the stricture of *Ra'abad* ad loc! Maimonides is consistent here with Guide 3:40. See also Blidstein, *Ekronot Mediniyyim BeMishnat HaRambam*, pp. 123, 132 n. 46.

41. *H. Rozeah* 4:8–9, and note 37. See also *H. Yesodei HaTorah* 8:2 (which, incidentally, is also a topos in Islamic legal theory).

42. See Blidstein, *Ekronot Mediniyyim BeMishnat HaRambam*, pp. 123–37.

43. *H. Rozeah* 2:2; here Maimonides sets the terminological code which is used in the following chapters of *H. Rozeah*.

44. *Ekronot Mediniyyim BeMishnat HaRambam*, pp. 75–90.

45. A.L. Feldman, ed., *Derashot HaRan* (Jerusalem: Makhon Shalem, 1977), pp. 189–90.

46. Rabbi Nissim was rapped on the knuckles for this entire exercise by Abrabanel to Deuteronomy 17: Abrabanel, a vigorous antimonarchist, had his own reasons for being sensitive to this expansion of monarchic power. For a recent, incisive treatment of Rabbi Nissim see A. Ravitzki, "Al Melakhim U-Mishpatim," in R. Bonfil et al., eds., *Tarbut VeHevrah BeToledot Yisrael Biymei HaBenayyim* (Jerusalem, 1989), pp. 469–82.

47. This idea goes back, ultimately, to Plato, *Republic* 1:351c; Rabbi Nissim attributes it here to "the sage." See R.A. Markus, *Saeculum: History and Society in the Theology of St. Augustine* (Cambridge: Cambridge University Press, 1970), pp. 22–153.

48. Feldman, *Derashot HaRan*, p. 190.

49. Ibid., p. 191.

50. In general, "R. Nissim's sermons are of a decidedly anti-philosophical character" (L. Feldman, "Nissim of Gerona," *Encyclopedia Judaica* 12:1186).

51. *Kuzari* 2:27; see G. Blidstein, "On Political Structures," *Jewish Journal of Sociology*, 22, no. 1 (June 1980): 54–55.

52. Feldman, *Derashot HaRan*, pp. 192–93.

53. Ibid., p. 194. For the history of this reading of Deuteronomy 17, see *Ekronot Mediniyyim BeMishnat HaRambam*, pp. 168–77.

54. Feldman, *Derashot HaRan*, p. 202.

55. In addition to the model presented in the text and discussed above, Rabbi Nissim also presents the following secondary model: "It may also be said that any matter related to the [religious] commands of the Torah, whether it is to be decided according to true justice or not, is within the jurisdiction of the court; and that in what concerns men alone—true justice alone is within the authority of the court . . . but what goes beyond that is given to the king to achieve." This, of course, reflects a reading of the traditional Jewish concepts *bein adam lehavero* and *bein adam lamakom* in political terms derived from the Christian *regnum* and *sanctum*. For other instances of this phenomenon, see G. Blidstein, "On Political Structures—Four Medieval Comments," *Jewish Journal of Sociology*, 15, no. 1 (June 1980): 47–59.

56. For the fourteenth-century Civilians, see R.W. and A.J. Carlyle, *A History of Medieval Political Theory in the West*, VI (repr. Edinburgh: Blackwood, 1962), pp. 76–82; cf. V, p. 99. For Philip the Fair and Boniface, see B. Tierney, *The Crisis of the Church and State* (Englewood Cliffs, NJ: Prentice-Hall, 1964), pp. 172–79; see, in general, B. Tierney, "The Prince Is Not Bound by the Law—Accursius and the Origins of the Modern State," *Comparative Studies in Society and History*, 5 (1963): 378–400. My thanks are due to my colleague Prof. Elena Lourie, who directed me to the discussions of Tierney.

57. I am again grateful to Prof. Lourie, for pointing this out to me. In the

"Privileges of Union" (1287) Alfonso III granted wide governmental privileges, including, eventually, the right of deposition, to the nobles of Aragon who had formed a union in defense of their rights during the reign of his father, Pedro III. See R.B. Merriman, *The Rise of the Spanish Empire*, I (New York: Macmillan, 1918), pp. 438–46, 459–66, 472–73; for the right of deposition, see p. 439. For a succinct discussion of the constitutional issues, see A. Mackay, *Spain in the Middle Ages* (New York: St. Martin's Press, 1977), pp. 104–6. See also M.L. Madden, *Political Theory and Law in Medieval Spain* (New York, 1930), pp. 101–23, 164–67. Ran's dates are given by Feldman as c.1290–c.1380.

58. Daniel Gutenmacher, "Political Obligation in the Thirteenth-Century Hispano-Jewish Community" (doctoral dissertation, New York University, 1986), pp. 187–88.

59. G. Blidstein, "Individual and Community in the Middle Ages: Halakhic Theory," in *Kinship and Consent*, ed. D. Elazar (Ramat Gan: Turtledove Press, 1981), pp. 224–25.

60. Elon, *Hamishpat Halvri*, I, pp. 42–45. In a sense, Elon is in search of a halakhic model that would legitimate state sovereignty, a difficult task in a theocentric system; see F. Hinsley, *Sovereignty*, 2nd ed. (Cambridge: Cambridge University Press, 1986).

61. This problem has been recently touched upon by J. Katz, in "The Middle Ages in Jewish History" (in Hebrew) in M. Bar-Asher, ed., *Mehkarim Be-Yahadut* (Jerusalem: Hebrew University, 1986), p. 217. D. Pipes's suggestion in *In the Path of God* that the national character of Judaism prevented the demoralization that he and others find in Islam, seems to me overly general, and a very partial explanation at best. It is also possible that Jews attributed this imperfect jurisprudential situation to their exilic condition, a fact for which the legal system itself could hardly be held responsible.

Medieval Jewish Political Institutions

The Foundations of Their Authority

ROBERT CHAZAN

Superficial perusal of Jewish political history has often resulted in a sense of two major modes of Jewish political life: thorough Jewish sovereignty, along the lines of the contemporary state of Israel, and a relative lack of Jewish political organization, or, more precisely, a lack of duly constituted Jewish political authority, along the lines of the contemporary American Jewish community and other present-day diaspora Jewries. Closer reading of the Jewish past, however, quickly indicates that these two paradigms fail to exhaust the totality of Jewish political experience. In fact they represent the unusual rather than the usual forms of Jewish political organization. At least two other major forms of political organization are more widely encountered in Jewish history than the two noted above: the dependent and limited sovereignty that characterized long stretches of Jewish history in the land of Israel (e.g., Jewish political dependence and limited sovereignty under the rule of Assyria, Babylonia, Ptolemaic Egypt, Seleucid Syria, and Rome) and the official autonomy that characterized most diaspora Jewish life until the advent of modern emancipation. In many ways, dependent and limited Jewish autonomy in the land of Israel and official autonomy in diaspora Jewry are closer to one another in central characteristics than either is to the two modern paradigms noted first. The purpose of this chapter is to investigate the foundations of Jewish communal autonomy in premodern diaspora Jewries.[1] The data utilized will be taken exclusively from early Ashkenazic Jewry, the Jewish community most familiar to me. It is clear, however, that similar material is available for other premodern Jewries and that the conclusions drawn from the Ashkenazic data are normative rather than idiosyncratic.[2]

Medieval Jewish communities were hardly independent and sovereign, as is the contemporary state of Israel; at the same time they were also not voluntary associations, as are contemporary diaspora Jewries. In fact, the considerable authority of the medieval Jewish community drew its strength from three separate but intertwined sources: the support of the non-Jewish political establishment, the needs of the Jewish community as a minority group living in threatening circumstances, and the sanctions of Jewish religious tradition. These separate sources of authority tended generally to reinforce one another; on occasion, of course, they could work against one another. We must attempt, first of all, to say a word about each of these three sources of communal authority, with heaviest emphasis on the first because it is often neglected.

Premodern societies in general, and the northern European society upon which we are focusing in particular, exhibited two characteristics that encouraged official governmental sanction for Jewish communal authority. The first was a tendency toward compartmentalization and the second was a tendency toward minimalism on the part of the ruling authorities. By the first I mean the tendency in premodern societies to recognize a multiplicity of constituent groups within a given society. As is well known, many medieval states were simply conglomerates of independent geographic areas, each with its own set of rules and institutions. What is true with regard to geography was similarly true for social groupings as well. A variety of groupings enjoyed substantial autonomy in most premodern states. One has only to bring to mind, for example, prerevolutionary France with its separate estates. The minimalist posture of premodern governments means the tendency to do as little as possible and to exploit as fully as possible those institutions already capable of affording necessary services. As an example, we might adduce the enormous social and educational role of the Roman Catholic Church in premodern European states, a reflection of governmental willingness to let ecclesiastical institutions shoulder a wide variety of societal burdens. Both of these characteristics of premodern societies worked to the advantage of extensive Jewish autonomy. In a society in which many groups enjoyed wide-ranging autonomy, substantial Jewish political separatism fit in well with general norms;

Jews had to receive no special dispensations for controlling their own affairs. Moreover, governments were fully prepared to allow Jews to do so; indeed they were delighted to exploit Jewish desire and capacity for self-rule.

As a result of these two broad characteristics of society and government, Jews were empowered to control many facets of Jewish communal life, with the understanding that the authorities would stand behind the decisions of the duly empowered agents of the Jewish community. This meant that there was more involved than simply voluntarism; the non-Jewish authorities delegated, as it were, to the Jewish community the right and responsibility to handle a range of issues in Jewish living. This is expressed nicely in the eleventh-century charter of invitation extended by Bishop Rüdiger of Speyer to Mainz Jews whom he invited to settle in his town, the earliest such charter that we possess for rapidly developing northern Europe. Interested in attracting Jews to his town, Bishop Rüdiger extended a "status more generous than any which the Jewish people have in any city of the German kingdom." Among the central provisions of this generous charter is the following:

> Just as the mayor of the city serves among the burghers, so too shall the Jewish leader [*archisynagogus*] adjudicate any quarrel which might arise among them or against them. If he be unable to determine the issue, then the case shall come before the bishop of the city or his chamberlain.[3]

This is an important stipulation. Just as the bishop had earlier delegated some of his judicial power to the Christian municipality, so he now delegated some of his authority to the Jewish community, or more precisely, to the leadership of that Jewish community. Where these leaders reached the limits of their capacities, the authority reverted to the bishop who had delegated it.

In order to buttress our conclusions, let us attend, again briefly, to follow-up legislation enacted for the Jewish community of Speyer a scant six years later, this time by the Emperor Henry IV.

> If the Jews have a dispute or a case among themselves to be decided, they shall be judged and convicted by their peers and by none other. If any wicked one among them wishes to hide the truth of an internal affair, he shall be forced, according to their law, by him who stands in

charge of the synagogue by appointment of the bishop to confess the truth of the matter in question. If difficult issues or disputes are raised among them or against them, they shall be referred to the presence of the bishop—their peace being preserved in the meantime—so that they might be settled by his judgment.[4]

While the thrust of this clause is the same as that encountered in Rüdiger's charter, it is useful in emphasizing a number of issues, two of special interest to us. The first is the utilization of force. The delegation of authority includes the use of coercion, for in truth without such power of coercion communal authority is nonexistent. Also of interest—and we shall return to this matter—is the reference to the norms of Jewish law. The emperor indicates the expectation that the behavior of the Jewish leadership to which political power has been delegated will be in accordance with the norms of Jewish law.

The focus in both of these documents that we have cited is delegation of judicial power—a matter of considerable concern to the Jews and their lords. An issue of equally great or perhaps greater importance to both the rulers of northern Europe and their Jewish subjects was taxation. Here again we encounter recurrently a delegation of authority. The Jews are made responsible for assessing and collecting the monies owed to the non-Jewish authorities. In view of the centrality of tax revenues as an incentive toward sponsoring Jewish settlement, the significance of easy access to such tax revenues looms large. In effect, tax income from the Jewish community cost nothing. The Jews themselves were saddled with total responsibility for assessing and collecting the requisite sums. In a setting in which rulers were often willing to part with substantial revenue in order to collect taxes (e.g., through the costly vehicle of tax farming), the total profit accruing from the Jewish community was surely inviting. Interestingly, governmental documents from tenth- and eleventh-century northern Europe make almost no reference to this important aspect of the relationship between the Jews and their rulers. By the twelfth and thirteenth centuries, however, there is ample reflection of the taxation of Jews through their communities in the increasingly copious governmental documentation, especially from the advanced states of England and France.[5] Rabbinic responsa even from the early period refer recurrently to issues that arose from the Jewish community's responsibility for assessing and collecting the sums owed to the non-Jewish authorities.[6]

One element in the power of the Jewish communal establishment was the backing of the non-Jewish authorities; a second was the perceived Jewish need to band together in the face of a hostile society. There was surely a sense among the Jews of northern Europe that only by pooling their resources could they maximize their political leverage. Given the precarious circumstances of Jewish existence, maximizing political leverage was crucial to Jewish survival. Unfortunately, neither non-Jewish nor Jewish sources dwell on this foundation of Jewish communal authority. Nonetheless, the basic need for cohesion was surely profoundly felt within the small Jewish enclaves of northern Europe. When we encounter the leadership of a medieval Jewish community or a set of such communities undertaking energetic political negotiations with the secular or political authorities on behalf of their confrères, the power to pursue such negotiations lay, in part, in a recognition of the absolute necessity for utilitarian political organization.[7] Even in more normal and stable circumstances, awareness of the pressing political and social need for cooperation operated as a central source for communal authority.

The third of the foundations of Jewish communal authority is relatively easy to describe. The premodern conception of Jewish law was extremely broad, covering all aspects of the Jew's individual and group experience. A crucial element in this far-reaching set of legal regulations related to the organization of the Jewish community. To be sure, within the vast complex of Jewish law, there were varying degrees of specificity—in certain areas the law was spelled out in minute detail; in others it was left relatively vague and general and thereby amenable to the fluctuations of human experience. One area, for example, in which the law remains fairly vague has to do with intra-family responsibilities. While generalizations are provided (e.g., the responsiblities of parents to children and children to parents), there is no effort to prescribe in the same manner as done, for example, in the dietary laws. The same tendency toward vagueness and elasticity is notable in the area of community reponsibility to the individual and individual responsibility to the community.[8] Here too there are recurrent generalizations, but no real effort to spell out in minute detail tax procedures, methods of enforcing discipline, or criteria for the selection of leaders. This latitude left room for different communities to adapt their procedures to the exigencies of varying times and places. Nonetheless, there was no lack of broad guidance and in particular no question as to the underlying religious foundation of Jewish community life. A Jew who flaunted the authority of his or her community was surely seen to be breaking the law in precisely the same way that he or she would be breaking the law by violating fundamental Sabbath ordinances or dietary restrictions.

These three separate sources of power in the Jewish community gave rise to diverse sanctions and to varying leadership groups. Brief discussion of each is in order. The three sources of power in Jewish communal life implied three different sets of sanctions imposed on recalcitrant Jews by the duly empowered authorities. Let us begin with the third foundation of power, Jewish law, and work our way backwards. The sanctions resulting from the inclusion of communal life and organization within the complex of Jewish law were of course religious. In one sense these sanctions were weak, for rarely did they involve a specific social or economic penalty. It would be a mistake, however, to overlook the enormous impact of these sanctions. In a society where the commitment to living according to the dictates of Jewish law was extremely high, the assertion that a certain set of behaviors ran counter to the demands of Jewish law had powerful impact. Rarely would a Jew be prepared, in such a society, to declare publicly a willingness to rebel against the dicates of Jewish law. Of course, the lack of specificity that we have already noted in this area of Jewish law provided latitude for the recalcitrant Jew to claim that he was in no sense rebelling against Jewish law; generally Jews challenging the dictates of communal leadership would claim that authority was being abused by the duly empowered leadership of the Jewish community and that their own behavior in no way contravened the demands of the law.

The recognized need for social cohesion led in a different direction. Here the communal leadership could exploit the perceived need for such cohesion through the medium of the ban of excommunication. Whatever the theoretical foundations of this ban, the mechanism itself represented exploitation by the leadership of the broadly perceived need for and concern with social cohesion. In effect, the ban of excommunication involved the extension of communal authority over those members of the community unwilling to acknowledge the powers of the Jewish political leadership through control of those who did acknowledge this leadership. The vehicle for this assertion of authority was the profound need that individual Jews had for the collectivity. By outlawing contact with recalcitrant Jews, the leadership of the Jewish community in effect exercised its authority over oppositional Jews through its control of the rest of the community. Given the structure of premodern social life, the result was an extremely powerful sanction, one that threatened from many perspectives the ostracized Jew.

As always, however, such weaponry had to be utilized sparingly and carefully: it could be exceedingly effective or thoroughly counterproductive. There were a number of dangers associated with invocation of the ban of excommunication. Let us focus on two. The first was the possibility of noneffectiveness. The ban was utilized as a result of weakness on the part of communal leadership. Individual Jews flaunted the authority of the community's leaders. If the effort were then made to bring the recalcitrant Jews to heel by invoking authority over those members of the community not in opposition, then the leadership ran the risk of having its weakness further exposed. Significant unwillingness to abide by the ban of excommunication would reveal yet greater weakness on the part of the heads of the community. At the other extreme was the possibility of too great an effectiveness of the ban of excommunication. The purpose of cutting an individual Jew off from contact with the rest of the community was to bring him to heel. There inevitably lurked the possibility that a zealously enforced ban of excommunication could lead the recalcitrant Jew to break his or her ties with the Jewish community. There is, for example, an interesting report that the thirteenth-century apostate Nicholas Donin, who did incalculable harm to European Jewry through his attack on the Talmud, was first set on this negative course by a ban of excommunication enacted against him.[9] In sum, the leadership of the Jewish community possessed a powerful weapon in the ban, but one that had to be utilized with extreme caution, lest it prove relatively ineffective or on occasion too effective.

The third foundation of Jewish communal authority, the support of the non-Jewish rulers, provided yet another set of sanctions, in some ways potentially the most effective of all. The non-Jewish rulers could conceivably put all of their force at the disposal of the Jewish communal leadership. For a number of obvious reasons, the leadership of the Jewish community had to be most reluctant to call for such assistance. In the first place, the call for outside assistance exposed to these important outside eyes the weakness of the Jewish leadership that it supported. This in itself was a dangerous message to communicate.

Moreover, intrusion of the non-Jewish authorities into the affairs of the Jewish community set a dangerous precedent: one could not predict where such intrusion, once initiated, might end. There is an interesting reflection in an early Ashkenazic responsum of reluctance to resort to the powerful sanction of direct non-Jewish intervention. Faced with the unwillingness of two members of a particular Jewish community to shoulder their share of the tax burden, the leadership of that community had decreed a ban of excommunication against these two Jews. This ban was abrogated by Jews in a neighboring community, who hosted the recalcitrant Jews and gave them a written release from the ban.

> When they [the two recalcitrant Jews] returned to Tiberias [a designa-
> tion for their original home community], they made public proclama-
> tion and exonerated themselves with respect to the matter. When the
> people of T heard this, they were enraged. They intended to tell the king
> to order his officials to seize his tax revenue. [They were prepared to do
> so out of a sense] that the powers of the community were being under-
> mined, for in effect they would enact and others could come and abro-
> gate. Subsequently they reconsidered [and they decided] to inquire as to
> whether their original decree still stood and whether the abrogation of
> the community of Sepphoris [a designation for the second community
> involved in the affair] was valid.[10]

This is a most interesting look into the affairs of a Jewish community. For our specific purposes at this juncture, it is unfortunate that we are not informed as to the precise reasons for the hesitation to call in royal power. All we are told is that the initial intention to seek the direct intervention of the non-Jewish authorities was reconsidered and was replaced by pursuit of the matter within the framework of Jewish law. While the precise thinking of these Jews is not specified, it seems likely that the considerations I have advanced—exposure of weakness to outside eyes and the danger of further and unwarranted intervention in internal Jewish affairs—may well have moved them to refrain from appealing directly for royal support.

Just as the varying foundations of Jewish communal authority gave rise to varying sanctions, so too did they produce a diversity of leader-ship elements within the Jewish community. Again, let us begin with the third source of communal authority and work backwards. The rootedness of Jewish communal authority in Jewish law made the rabbinic interpreters of that law figures of paramount importance in Jewish communal leadership. Put differently, inclusion of community activity within the complex of Jewish law made that communal activity as amenable to rabbinic leadership as was every other facet of Jewish life. The rabbis, by virtue of their command of Jewish law, had to play a major role in the affairs of the community that was so heavily anchored in that law. Once more the vagueness of Jewish law in the area of communal organization vitiated somewhat the power of the rabbis in this area; it did not, however, nullify such power. Far from it. Rabbinic authority constituted a considerable force, which had to be reckoned with.

The need for social cohesion and the realities of Jewish economic life inevitably brought another leadership group to the fore, the elite of wealth and power. The power of this elite was based on a number of factors. In the first place, the wealthy were inevitably employers of others within the Jewish community. Thus, a variety of poorer Jews were beholden to the wealthy, and in many ways subservient. Moreover, there was a strong sense in premodern society in general that political power should be commensurate with level of tax contribution: the larger the contribution, the greater the corresponding political influence should be. Jews clearly shared this sense. Indeed in the Jewish communities, this notion was realistic: large contributors had in fact to be appeased. Wealthy Jews offended by the policies of a given Jewish community could betake themselves elsewhere, thereby depriving that Jewish community of a significant part of its resources.

Finally, the reality of non-Jewish support for Jewish political authority gave special power to those few Jews who had direct links to the non-Jewish world. To be sure, the group involved was more or less the wealthy elite in any case. In the Ashkenazic world, business dealings and wealth were the only significant means of fashioning links with the non-Jewish establishment. In any case, the reality of close contact with precisely those non-Jewish authorities whose support was so vital to the workings of the Jewish community inevitably thrust such Jews into positions of substantial power within the Jewish fold.

Under the best of circumstances, these three foundations of Jewish communal authority—the support of the non-Jewish rulers, the need for social cohesion, and the religious validation broadly articulated in Jewish law—reinforced each other. We have already noted one example of such reinforcement, Emperor Henry IV's assumption that the coercion by Jewish communal leadership that he was supporting would of course be in accordance with the dictates of Jewish law. When these three sources of authority reinforced one another, the result was enormous power for the duly constituted leadership of the Jewish community. Under optimal conditions, the two leadership groupings—the rabbinic experts and the elite of wealth and political connections— worked amicably together. Indeed there is some indication that, on occasion, one and the same family or individual would incorporate the diverse leadership characteristics that we have noted. Rabbi Jacob Tam, the grandson of Rashi and the decisive early figure among the Tosafists, was reputed to be much more than a distinguished master of Jewish law; he was supposed to have been quite wealthy and in direct contact with the highest political authorities in northern France.[11] It seems clear that the varying foundations of Jewish political power often reinforced each other quite effectively and that the diverse leadership elements were often capable of harmonious cooperation.

It is not surprising, however, that effective reinforcement and harmonious cooperation were not always the rule. Given the diversity that we have depicted, it is almost predictable that on occasion conflicts of interests and perspectives could and did erupt in medieval Ashkenazic Jewry, as they did elsewhere in the Jewish world. The rabbinic authorities and the elite of wealth did not always see eye to eye. Among early Ashkenazic Jewry there was a palpable fear that well-connected Jews would manipulate their political leverage to advantage. A recurring theme in Jewish communal legislation was the need for limiting exploitation of connections to the non-Jewish authorities. Such limitation is one of the central motifs in the illuminating tax legislation attributed to Rabbi Solomon ben Isaac of Troyes (Rashi). This enactment reaffirmed the generalized responsibility of each individual Jew to share the fiscal burdens of the community and repudiated any non-Jewish interference in this shared burden, interference gained by individual approach to the non-Jewish rulers.[12] The same concern is manifested in a yet more impressive ordinance enacted by the grandsons of Rashi, Rabbi Jacob Tam and Rabbi Samuel ben Meir. Let us cite only the central paragraph, which enunciates the underlying principle.

> We have further decreed, ordained, and proclaimed under threat of excommunication that no one be permitted to gain power over his fellow through a king, an officer, or a judge, in such a way as to punish,

fine, or coerce [his fellow]. [This applies to] both secular and sacred matters.

The concern is obvious. Individual Jews well connected with the non-Jewish authorities might abuse those links in order to further their own affairs, at the expense of individual fellow-Jews or of the Jewish community as a whole. Given the complex sources of power in Jewish affairs, such abuse was alarming and highly threatening.

The political life of premodern Ashkenazic Jewry, and by extension of premodern Jewry in general, was far from simple. The sources of authority were diverse, giving rise to a range of sanctions and a variety of leadership groups. These complexities could often lead in the direction of weakness, through both external interference and internal friction. More often, however, the same complexities led to relative strength, with the diverse foundations of power and authority effectively reinforcing one another. The challenges generated by minority status in a fairly hostile environment were immense. The self-governing structure that we have analyzed was one of the prime elements in the capacity of premodern Jewries to cope with the difficult circumstances confronting them.

Notes

1. The classic treatment of premodern Jewish self-government is to be found in Salo W. Baron, *The Jewish Community*, 3 vols. (Philadelphia: The Jewish Publication Society of America, 1948), vol. I, pp. 157–374. Baron reformulated his findings in *A Social and Religious History of the Jews*, 18 vols. (New York: Columbia University Press, 1952), vol. V, pp. 3–81. Also important is Louis Finkelstein, *Jewish Self-Government in the Middle Ages* (New York: Jewish Theological Seminary of America, 1920). Two additional studies of prime significance are: Yitzhak Baer, "The Origins of the Organization of the Jewish Community of the Middle Ages" (Hebrew), *Zion* XV (1950): 1–41, and Gerald Blidstein, "Individual and Community in the Middle Ages: Halakhic Theory," in *Kinship and Consent: The Jewish Political Tradition and Its Contemporary Uses*, ed. Daniel J. Elazar (Washington, DC: University Press of America, 1983), pp. 215–56. The copious notes in the Blidstein article introduce the reader to valuable recent literature on the topic. The Finkelstein, Baer, and Blidstein studies are based ultimately on the extant halakhic materials. As research into the notarial records of southern Europe progresses, new perspectives on Jewish community life are afforded. For two examples of these new perspectives, see Joseph Shatzmiller, *Recherches sur la communauté juive de Manosque au moyen âge* (Paris, 1973), pp. 33–63, and idem, "L'excommunication, la communauté juive et

les autorités temporelles au moyen âge," *Les Juifs dan l'histoire de France*, ed. Myriam Yardeni (Leiden: E.J. Brill, 1980), pp. 63–69. The present study is intended merely to sketch in broad strokes somes of the central issues associated with the study of premodern Jewish communal organization.

2. The fullest statement on early Ashkenazic Jewry and its patterns of communal organization is to be found in Irving A. Agus, *The Heroic Age of Franco-German Jewry* (New York: Yeshiva University Press, 1969), pp. 185–276. Agus published two volumes of early Ashkenazic rabbinic responsa, topically organized. For material on Jewish community organization, see idem, *Urban Civilization in Pre-Crusade Europe*, 2 vols. (New York: Yeshiva University Press, 1968), vol. II, pp. 421–553. Both the Baer and the Blidstein studies noted above focus on materials from early Ashkenazic Jewry, as is the case in the present essay. As research progresses, it will be important to gain a sense of the distinctiveness of various sets of premodern Jewish communities.

3. Alfred Hilgard, ed., *Urkunden zur Geschichte der Stadt Speyer* (Strassburg: Trübner, 1885), pp. 11–12. Throughout this paper all English translations will be my own. For an English translation of the entire document, see Robert Chazan, *Church, State, and Jew in the Middle Ages* (New York: Behrman House, 1980), pp. 58–59.

4. Hilgard, *Urkunden zur Geschichte der Stadt Speyer*, pp. 12–14. An English translation of the entire document can be found in Chazan, *Church, State, and Jew in the Middle Ages*, pp. 60–63.

5. Both the Speyer documents lack any significant reference to taxation. The latter charter says nothing whatsoever on the issue. The former mentions an annual payment of three and a half pounds to the monks of the town in return for the land given to the Jews for their settlement. The Jewish tax in Speyer surely went beyond that sum. For substantial evidence of taxation of Jews in twelfth- and thirteenth-century England, see Cecil Roth, *A History of the Jews in England*, 3rd ed. (Oxford: Oxford University Press, 1964), pp. 18–90; H. G. Richardson, *The English Jews under Angevin Kings* (London: Methuen, 1960), pp. 135–75; Robert C. Stacy, *Politics, Policy, and Finance under Henry III, 1216–1245* (Oxford: Oxford University Press, 1987), passim. For twelfth- and thirteenth-century France, see my *Medieval Jewry in Northern France* (Baltimore: Johns Hopkins University Press, 1973), passim.

6. Note, for example, the discussion by Agus in his *Heroic Age of Franco-German Jewry*, pp. 232–40, and the rabbinic materials that he cites.

7. For an interesting example of extensive political negotiations carried on by the leadership of early Ashkenazic Jewry, see my "The Blois Incident of 1171: A Study in Jewish Intercommunal Organization," *Proceedings of the American Academy for Jewish Research*, 36 (1968): 13–31.

8. This is the cental issue addressed in the excellent Blidstein study referred to in note 1. Again the notes are copious and direct the reader to relevant literature.

9. Two Jewish sources mention this excommunication and its results. The first is Rabbi Yehiel of Paris, in his account of the proceedings in Paris in 1240: *Vikuah Rabbenu Yehiel mi-Pariz*, ed. Reuven Margolies (Lwow, 1928), p. 13. The second and later reference is found in the letter of Jacob ben Eli of Venice; see the letter as edited by Joseph Kobak in *Jeschurun* VI (1868): Heb. sec., p. 29.

10. *Teshuvot Maharam bar Baruch*, ed. Raphael Rabinowitz (Lwow, 1860), p. 43b, no. 423. For an English translation of the entire document, see Agus, *Urban Civilization in Pre-Crusade Europe*, vol. II, 466–68, no. cliii.

11. On Rabbi Jacob Tam, see the full exposition in Ephraim E. Urbach, *Ba' aley ha-Tosafot*, 4th ed. (Jerusalem: Mossad Bialik, 1980), vol. I, pp. 60–113.

12. *Teshuvot Rashi*, ed. Israel Elfenbein (New York, 1943), pp. 290–91.

13. The Hebrew text can be found in Finkelstein, *Jewish Self-Government in the Middle Ages*, pp. 152–55. A complete English translation appears on pp. 155–58.

Modern Jewish Politics East and West (1840–1939)

Utopia, Myth, Reality

JONATHAN FRANKEL

The Concept of Bipolarity: East and West

The systematic study of Jewish politics as a major theme in Jewish history has been gaining rapid momentum over the last decades. Jewish historiography first developed in the nineteenth century predominantly as the history of ideas and, although this approach soon lost its monopoly, it has remained of central importance ever since. Scholem not only rebelled against Graetz, but also followed in his footsteps. However, partly in direct reaction to *Ideengeschichte*, new schools associated with Simon Dubnov, Salo Wittmayer Baron, Raphael Mahler, and Jacob Katz, for example, chose to focus their research on the social and economic history of the Jews.

Thus, the contemporary rise of political history represents yet another turn of the wheel. Since World War II, the stream of political biographies; of party, movement, and organizational histories; of diplomatic studies; and now, increasingly, of works focused on politics as a central strand running through the history of the Jewish people as a whole,[1] has flowed ever stronger. What is more, political science, its methods and concepts, has stamped its mark on many of the most recent publications.

There are two separate developments involved here. First, it has to be recalled that the study of politics was long understood to mean essentially the study of government, public law, and international diplomacy. Today, though, political scientists examine the workings of power and influence at all levels of society. The politics of gender, of the family, of voluntary associations, of ethnic groups and interethnic relations are all treated as important objects of research. Under these circumstances it is only natural that the distribution of power within the Jewish community, on the one hand, and the relationship of the community to the various external power centers, on the other, are now treated as a legitimate and key area of study where history and political science overlap.

Far more significant, however, is the fact that political thought and action have combined to transform the situation of the Jewish people in the world so totally over the last two centuries—and particularly, over the last fifty years. The geographic distribution, the socioeconomic structure, and the cultural differentiation characteristic of the Jewish people today are the direct result, above all else, of developments set in motion by the English, American, French, Russian, Nazi, and Zionist revolutions.

Less than seventy years ago, Franz Rosenzweig could still advance the view, very commonly held in the nineteenth century, that it was the destiny of the Jews to exist "outside History." But, in the meantime, the Jewish people has not only been made over, and almost exterminated, by history, political history, but has also itself made history, creating its own state, *ex nihilo*, as it were.

Rarely has the role of politics as an autonomous factor of great weight in the process of change been so dramatically demonstrated. Historiography, the current perception of the past, almost always bears the stamp of the present, of immediate and recent experience, and so in the postwar years Jewish history has been written primarily (although not exclusively) as political history—even though this has meant swimming against those dominant intellectual fashions that have favored structuralist, sociological, and quantifiable methods.

One of the most fundamental assumptions that has shaped the analysis of modern Jewish history is the belief that emergent Jewish politics followed two distinct, indeed opposite, patterns of development—the Western and the East European. This concept of a basic bifurcation is familiar enough.

On the one hand—and this is the accepted image—the brand of politics developed during the nineteenth and early twentieth centuries by the Jews in France, England, Germany, and the United States was strictly limited in its aims and its means. To define the Jewish people in terms of religion, and to deny its character as a nationality, meant of necessity to confine political action to high-minded, appropriate issues. To work for equal rights, for emancipation; to advance the health, education, and welfare of their "co-religionists"; to refute and discredit anti-Semitic accusations (all this at home and abroad)—these were the goals set for themselves by the leadership of Western Jewry. Political lobbying, public advocacy, and philanthropy were the methods preferred. The modes of organization tended toward the oligarchic, in practice, if not always in theory; and the day-to-day execution of decisions was left largely to a paid officialdom.

Realism, caution, tact, a careful empiricism, and a strict accounting were the hallmarks of this political style. Change for the better was expected almost as a matter of faith, but it would come in evolutionary, incrementalist, ameliorative fashion. In sum, this was the pattern developed variously by Moses Montefiore and Adolphe Crémieux, Paul Nathan and Eduard Fuchs, Jacob Schiff and Louis Marshall; by the Board of Deputies and the Anglo-Jewish Association; by the Consistoire Centrale and the Alliance Israélite Universelle; by the Centralverein and the Hilfsverein; by the American Jewish Committee and the Joint Distribution Committee.[2] It was the Western "subsystem" of Jewish politics.

For their part (again according to the received wisdom), the East European Jews developed a radically different type of political culture. Their definition of Jewish peoplehood as national, not religious, in nature had implications of the most radical kind. Nationhood inevitably carried with it, in the modern world at least, a latent claim to national self-determination—a separate political and cultural existence. Minimally, this meant that the Russian and Austrian empires would have to be reconstructed as a federation of nationalities in which the Jewish people would enjoy some form of national autonomy. More dramatically, it could be understood to mean that the Jews should undertake to establish their own state, either in Palestine or in some other, potentially more hospitable, territory. Maximally, it was often seen as synonymous with the idea of nothing less than the abolition of the Diaspora and the "ingathering of the exiles," all the Jewish people in their own state.

Political programs of this type were clearly revolutionary or quasi-revolutionary in nature, involving, as they did, the assumption that nothing less than systemic change could solve the Jewish question. Often, their goal was literally political—or even social—revolution: the overthrow of the tsarist regime and the establishment of a new order. But the idea of a modern Exodus was in many ways still more far-reaching and daring. Utopian and quasi-messianic visions were thus endemic to the East European style of politics, which sought another and higher reality concealed within—and about to replace—the flux of everyday actualities.

The contrast between the two systems, of course, went far beyond the realm of ideology. In Eastern Europe, the basic form of political organization was not the public committee but the party, or the movement, which aimed at the maximal mobilization of its membership, be it in the name of revolution or of the Exodus (or quite often of both). Leadership, in turn, was drawn in the main from the intelligentsia (meaning, variously, the university-educated, the autodidacts of Yeshiva background, or the "worker intelligentsia").

Here, then, was the political subculture developed variously by the Bilu and Am Olam movements, by Hibat Zion and the Russian Zionists, by the Bund and the Folkists; by Moshe Leb Lilienblum and Lev Pinsker; Simon Dubnov and Chaim Zhitlovsky; Arkadii Kremer and Vladimir Kossovsky; Abraham Lesin and A. Litvak; Berl Katznelson and David Ben Gurion.[3] Its negation of the present was inspired by a vision of a future where man and society would be made over anew.

The Limits of Bipolar Historiography

Presented in such a schematic way, this dichotomous analysis, although long accepted perhaps as axiomatic, naturally arouses suspicion as being too symmetrical, too neat—a caricature even—given the inevitable untidiness and intractibility of empirical reality. However, it is not our intention here to suggest that this primary theme is fundamentally flawed or that it has lost its utility. On the contrary, the "Western" and "East European" models can, if handled with care, be immensely useful in the analysis of emergent Jewish politics. At the same time, though, they can also be highly misleading unless set firmly in context and measured constantly against the actual chaos of historical change. Their use has to be qualified in many basic ways.

Thus, first, it should be remembered that the idea of the East–West division is not simply an analytical concept but has its own history, now going back over more than one hundred years, and cannot easily be freed from a past that is highly emotive and politically partisan. As early as the 1870s, Peretz Smolenskin, in a series of powerful articles in his Hebrew monthly, *Ha-shahar* (The Dawn), developed the idea that the Jewish Enlightenment (or Haskalah) movement in Western Europe had embarked on a path of national betrayal. The determination of Jews in the West to define themselves as Jewish by religion only and as Germans, Frenchmen, or Englishmen by nationality; their loss of interest in the Hebrew language; their readiness in many cases to discard ideas of national redemption (an eventual return to the national homeland) even from the prayer books—all added up in his view to a fundamental lack of patriotism, an abandonment of the ancestral heritage, to a shameful act of collective cowardice. In his famous article, "Am Olam" (The Eternal People),[4] he condemned Moses Mendelssohn and the "Berlin Haskalah" out of hand. Smolenskin demanded that the Enlightenment movement in Eastern Europe adopt a totally different path; seek an alternative synthesis between modernity and tradition; foster pride in Hebrew as a national, a living, language; treat the sacred works of Judaism as the basis of a new national literature; shun religious reform as a danger to national unity.

This vehement rejection of the Western path to modernity (already anticipated in part by Moses Hess in *Rome and Jerusalem*)[5] was to prove itself extraordinarily popular in tsarist Russia in the period 1881–1914 and in independent Poland and Lithuania between the wars. It appealed to many of the same emotions that gave Slavophile and *narodnik* (populist) ideas such a strong hold on the Russian intelligentsia[6] and fostered romantic nationalism in Central and Eastern Europe generally during the nineteenth century. Fear of intellectual and cultural domination by the economically advanced countries of the West, resentment of the "center" by the "periphery," of the "metropolis" by the "provinces" (to use the terminology of Edward Shils)[7] produced an inevitable reaction. The urge to maintain and develop a separate identity, more authentic, linked organically to national traditions and genuinely creative, constantly asserted itself.

With the rise of Jewish national movements from the 1880s, belief in the basic division between East and West became a source of great psychological strength. It was brilliantly encapsulated in Ahad Ha-Am's comparison of "the freedom in slavery" characteristic of Russian Jewry with "the slavery in freedom" to be found among the Western

Jews.[8] It did much to inspire the growth of newspaper and periodical publication, of high-quality literature and, in time, education in the Hebrew and Yiddish languages. It acted as a source of pride, self-confidence, and political creativity. The Western Jews, who often poured scorn on the "Ostjuden"—the "Polaken" and the "Galitsianer"[9]—were in turn condemned as (for the most part) "assimilationists" and (when engaged in political lobbying) as *shtadlonim* who went cap-in-hand to beg from the powers-that-be.

But, of course, like every political myth, this one, too, could not serve as an accurate guide to reality. In its play with fixed "essences," it suggested a static and permanent division. In its partisan enthusiasms, it was utterly one-sided and tended to pin the charge of "assimilationism" on a vast array of nonnationalists regardless of whether they were committed to, or against, Jewish survival. Invaluable as a political weapon, it has acted to distort Jewish historiography which has so often tended to neglect the independent political role of Western Jewry or to dismiss it as a transitory, dwarfed, or negative phenomenon. In sum, accumulated layers of myth have to be stripped away from the East–West dichotomy if it is to serve as a tool of analysis rather than of polemics.

The truth is that the division between the "assimilationist" West and the "nationalist" East was not "essential" but "existential," fluid, subject to the most dynamic processes of change. This was, in large part, due to the fact that Jewish ideologies, attitudes, and modes of behavior varied in response to the particular political system prevailing at any given moment in any given county (or region even). Thus, with the growth from the mid-nineteenth century of mass migration on a vast scale—within the states of Eastern and Central Europe, across frontiers, and from one continent to another—the political "subculture" of the Jews was thrown into a state of constant flux. Migration resulted, primarily, from economic pressures but, to some extent, also from political and cultural preferences. In this way, it not only produced, but also reflected, political transformations.

Within the tsarist empire, for example, St. Petersburg and Moscow saw the emergence of leadership groups that in every way fitted the "Western" model of Jewish politics. The only Jews who could legally settle in the capital cities were those belonging to the most select strata—primarily members of the First and Second Merchant Guilds, and university graduates. Emancipated to all effects and purposes themselves, and having chosen to move out of the Pale, they adopted the standard "emancipationist" strategies. The Society for the Dissemination of the Enlightenment (OPE) and the Society for Craft Training (ORT), set up in 1863 and 1880 respectively, were designed to equip the young generation of Jews to play a full and productive role in Russian society.[10] In the crisis of 1881–82, the St. Petersburg magnates, the Ginzburgs and the Poliakovs, vehemently opposed the emigrationist strategies then demanded by the proto-Zionist and proto-territorialist camps. The legitimacy of their leadership role in Russian Jewry was thereby severely undermined, but far from fully destroyed.[11]

Up until the 1917 revolutions this elite continued to serve as the key link to the elites of Western Jewry whether for the receipt and distribution of emergency relief funds or for the exchange of political advice. Joined by ties of friendship, mutual confidence, joint financial interests, and even, in some cases, by marriage, to the world of the Schiffs, Rothschilds, Swaythlings, and Warburgs, they actually represented an integral unit in the subsystem of Jewish politics that (however anomalously in this case) is associated with the West.

Again, the direct impact of the larger political context on the Jewish style of politics can be observed by comparing developments in the three different areas that together had constituted independent Poland until the partitions of 1772–1815. The forcing ground of maximalism in its various forms—revolutionary parties, plans for the Exodus, pioneering movements for Palestinian settlement—was the Pale of Settlement. Relentless pressure by the regimes of Alexander III and Nicholas II produced extreme, violent, and apocalyptic reactions.

In Galicia, part of the Austro-Hungarian Empire until 1918, the same political processes could be observed but in far less intense, much milder form. Thus, a sister party to the Bund was established in Galicia,[12] but it came late on to the scene (1905) and remained relatively weak throughout. Zionism gained support, but its orthodox-Marxist, pioneering, and maximalist offshoots were discernible only in the most atrophied forms. The Hapsburg regime, relatively popular among most of its Jewish citizens, did not foster the extremism so common across the frontier.

As for the Posen area, annexed to Prussia, there the Jews, in very large part, took the opportunity to migrate westward, above all to Berlin. Even those who remained came to see themselves, for the most part, as Germans by allegiance, alienated from the local Polish population, and Jewish by religion alone. This example of the "Western" model at work, far to the east geographically, was marked, of course, by the parallel and similar development in Hungary, where Jewish identification with the Magyar nationality and culture had taken very deep root by 1914.[13]

A somewhat different pattern, again, shaped the American experience. Some two million immigrants from Eastern Europe, primarily from the Russian empire, who arrived in the United States in the period 1881–1914, brought with them the politics of the Pale. Every party and every ideology familiar in Russia was replanted across the Atlantic. But even before World War I, it was obvious to all but the most blinkered observers that many of these seedlings could not take root in the new soil and were destined to wither away. Indeed, in making the decision to go to America in the first place, the immigrants usually realized that they had opted for a very different way of life.

In America, revolutionary maximalism (anarchism, for example), disciplined party organizations, and plans for Jewish national autonomy and education in the national languages (Hebrew and Yiddish) were forced into constant retreat. On the other hand, mass unionism and mass newspapers in Yiddish, both socialist and pro-Zionist, flourished. In fact, it was only in America that these phenomena, so very "Eastern" typologically, reached their full potential.

Once the gates were closed tight against further immigrants in 1924, however, the model of politics imported from Russia was doomed to atrophy. By the second or third generation, the descendants of the East European immigration—native speakers of English, fully aware of the benefits of equal citizenship and open economic opportunities—tended to accept the patterns of identity already established by the German-Jewish immigrants as part of the natural order of things. They were Jews by religion, but members of the American nation. More and more, East European Jews came to people, and even lead, the institutions originally considered typically "German": the Reform movement, the American Jewish Committee, the Joint. (And if there has been something of a reversal in attitudes since the 1970s, it is again due primarily to a change in the general political climate—this time, the swing toward ethnicity in the American civic consciousness).

However, beyond this particular issue (emphasizing the dynamic rather than the static), there is another fundamental problem: to what extent did East European Jewry, in reality, identify with the type of

Jewish politics described here as quintessentially East European? However paradoxical it may seem, it is not always possible to answer this question with any degree of certainty. Under the tsarist regime very few elections were held and they excluded large parts of the population from the franchise.[14] Moreover, the more traditional certain sections of the community were, the less likely they were to vote.

Existing historiography, itself so largely a product of the "new Jewish politics," clearly tends, in this case, too, to give a misleading impression by focusing on the innovative and revolutionary. Certainly, traditional Judaism, the authority of the Orthodox rabbis, the prestige of the *kheyder* and the *beys hamedrash*, and the alliance between "oligarchy" and "theocracy" (that is, between wealth and Talmudic learning) were thrown on the defensive throughout the period 1881–1939. By their very nature as highly conservative leaderships, they were slow to adopt new methods in order to protect their way of life, be it in the educational or the political sphere. And they were faced by an array of movements (nationalist, socialist, radical) that were passionately convinced that time and truth—scientific truth—were on their side.

Nonetheless, despite all the many handicaps, the Orthodox world proved able to maintain itself as a major force not only in tsarist Russia and Hapsburg Galicia, but also in Poland, Lithuania, and Romania between the wars. While a few of the rabbis were prepared to accept the legitimacy of Zionism and even join the Zionist organization,[15] most were adamantly opposed to secular politics in every shape and form. And there were vast areas in the Pale, Congress Poland, and Galicia from which modern Jewish politics was virtually excluded. The fact that these regions were, in the main, economically underdeveloped and plagued by poverty; that most Jews continued to live in small towns and to eke out a living as shopkeepers, petty traders, or artisans; and that very large numbers were dependent on community assistance in order to keep body and soul together—all tended to reinforce the traditional order. The areas of Hassidic dominance proved to be particularly inimical to modernizing forces.

Moreover, the Orthodox showed themselves to be quite capable of finding their own ways to exert effective political influence. They dominated the community councils (*kehilot*) in Congress Poland and Galicia before World War I, often in alliance with the antinationalist Jewish liberals (the so-called assimilationists) and in the face of the

Zionist efforts to wrest control at the periodic elections. And, more surprising, perhaps, this pattern largely persisted in interwar Poland. By then the Orthodox camp had organized its own party, Agudes Yisroel, which proved far more effective than any other Jewish movement in winning a measure of governmental backing.[16] And no less significant is the fact (emphasized by Ezra Mendelsohn) that in the mid-1930s the school system associated with Agude had more than twice as many pupils as the Zionist Tarbut and Yiddish Tsisho systems combined (110,000 as against slightly over 50,000).[17]

Of course, this is by no means the whole picture. Mainstream Zionism won handsome victories in the elections to the Polish Sejm in the postwar years, easily outpolling the other Jewish parties (winning 180,000 votes in 1919, for example, as against some 97,000 for the Orthodox).[18] This fact was very significant, but, in the context being discussed here, not quite as indicative as it might at first appear, for a large number of the Zionist votes undoubtedly came from religiously observant Jews who were quite out of tune with the modernizing leadership of the movement. In sum, the "new Jewish politics," for all its remarkable successes, was never able to sweep aside the formidable barriers presented by the traditional way of life and the traditional leaderships.

If the Hassidic world of Agude thus opposed Jewish nationalism in the name of tradition, and if acculturated liberals opposed it ("Western"-style) as damaging to the cause of emancipation, there were also many Jews who rejected it out of hand as insufficiently revolutionary or radical. In the early years of the century, over 30 percent of the revolutionaries arrested in the tsarist empire were Jews.[19] A large number of them belonged to Jewish movements, particularly to the Bund, but a high percentage were drawn from the general revolutionary parties—the Russian Social Democratic Labor Party (the SDs), the Party of Socialist Revolutionaries (the SRs), the Polish Socialist Party (PPS), and the Social Democratic Party of the Kingdom of Poland and Lithuania, to name only the most important.

For the most part, they defined themselves as "internationalists" and saw the solution to the Jewish question as the attainment of full civil rights and total integration. The term "assimilationist," so often used tendentiously, really did apply to most of the Jews in this particular category, who, being committed materialists, atheists, left-wing Nietzcheans, or simply root-and-branch antitraditionalists, considered

Judaism as a religion to be noxious and the idea of Jewish nationality to be a reactionary fiction.[20]

In numerical terms, revolutionaries of this type obviously constituted a miniscule percentage of the Jewish people. One is talking of a few thousand, after all. But, throughout, their significance in Jewish life and politics was vastly greater than their strength in numbers. The highly prominent role played by generations of revolutionary Jews—from Aron Zundelevich and Hessia Helfman at the time of the assassination of Alexander II, to Leon Trotsky, Karl Radek, and Rosa Luxemburg during the years of revolution and civil war—meant that the "internationalist" alternative to autonomous Jewish politics was always powerfully represented on the left. Movements that were both socialist and nationalist such as the Bund and the Poale Zion found themselves in direct and constant competition with the major revolutionary parties in Russia before 1917. And they formulated their ideological platforms in large part specifically to prove that their nationalism was compatible with orthodox Marxism.

With the victory of Bolshevism and the establishment of Jewish sections in the Communist parties of both Soviet Russia and independent Poland, the conflict became nakedly violent. All the major Jewish parties (whether socialist or not) were closed down in Soviet Russia by 1921, and many Bundists, socialist Zionists, and socialist territorialists chose to join the Evsektsiia, the Jewish section of the Russian Communist Party.[21] In the new Polish state, the Communist Party was declared illegal, but still attracted many young Jews; and the conflict between the Communists and the left-wing Jewish parties often seemed to become the more merciless the narrower the ideological gap between them.[22]

The fact that in Soviet Russia during the 1920s, a Yiddish culture (albeit in strictly Soviet "proletarian" form) was allowed to flourish and that anti-Semitism together with all forms of racial incitement was declared illegal made the Communist alternative a constant source of attraction, especially given the terrible economic and political problems facing the Jews in the newly independent states bordering the Soviet Union.

Ultimately and ironically, though, the polarization, the vicious circle, produced by anti-Semitism and the charges of a world Jewish conspiracy, on the one hand, and the flow of young Jews into the ranks of internationalist Marxism, on the other, probably served to reinforce

Jewish nationalism. The desire to escape the cauldron of Eastern Europe and build up a new homeland in Palestine produced an ever-growing stream of recruits to the Zionist pioneer movement; by 1933 He-halutz in Poland had, quite remarkably, close to sixty thousand members.[23]

Closely related to this issue of how far Eastern European Jewry actually identified itself with the "new" or "East European" model of Jewish politics was the question of whether the national movements actually did create a democratic alternative to the oligarchic principle which they associated with the West. Here the answer, necessarily much encapsulated, would seem to be that, in the main (the avowedly elitist groups apart), they were genuinely committed to the idea of mass mobilization, mass membership, and, in varying degrees, also to democratic structures and participation, but that a vast gap usually divided rhetoric from reality. Given the future-oriented and often utopian programs of the major movements (Zionism, the Bund, territorialism), it was much easier to attain peaks of momentary enthusiasm than to sustain day-to-day activism or even paid-up membership. The harsh economic climate did not encourage sustained voluntary work for, or payments to, political movements that promised, but could not produce, basic change.

It is for this reason that modern Jewish politics in Eastern Europe was marked by such extraordinary ebbs and flows. At moments of crisis, when the political movements and parties were perceived to have clear leadership roles, support and membership soared upwards. This was the case in 1881–82 (albeit in inchoate forms), in 1905–6, and in 1917. But when the vast expectations could no longer be sustained, support melted away at astonishing rates. Parties with tens of thousands of members in the Russia of 1906 could report only hundreds by 1909.[24]

The same phenomenon occurred in interwar Poland, although in less dramatic form, as there were no crises of comparable proportions. Thus, reports reveal a remarkable disparity between the number of "shekels" (nominal memberships) sold every few years at the time of Zionist congresses by the Polish Zionist Federation and the number of active members—162,000 for example, as opposed to some 2,000, in 1921.[25] No less indicative of the highly volatile nature of support were the violent swings in the fortunes of one party or another. The general Zionist movement, which had a predominant lead in the 1920s, went into rapid decline in the 1930s when the Revisionists under Vladimir Jabotinsky's lead made great gains. And the Bund, marginalized in the elections of the 1920s, could claim to be the largest Jewish party by the late 1930s.[26]

In the face of these realities, the political movements not infrequently felt compelled to modify the utopian nature of their policies. The mainstream Zionist organization, first in tsarist Russia and then in Poland, committed itself more and more to a dual program: on the one hand, participation in the construction of a Jewish homeland in Palestine, and on the other, participation in the struggle for national rights in Poland, including a national school system and economic amelioration (*Gegenwartsarbeit*). Similarly, the Bund, although always a would-be revolutionary Marxist party, gained much of its support in interwar Poland as a result of its sustained investment of effort in the Yiddish school movement, in trade unionism, and in the day-to-day struggle against anti-Semitic harassment.[27] In constrast, the Zionist pioneer movements (Ha-Shomer Ha-Tsair, Gordonia, Hehalutz) clearly opted for an elitist alternative, focusing their energies on the future, on the preparation for life as workers in Palestine.

All in all, then, it is hard to sustain the straigthforward claim that the new politics involved "democratization" and mass mobilization as opposed to the oligarchical principle characteristic of Jewish organization in the West. Indeed, it must remain doubtful whether any political movement in Eastern Europe was ever able to sustain over a period of many years a paid-up and regular membership comparable to that of a number of voluntary movements in the West such as, for example, the major Jewish defense organization, the Centralverein, in Germany, which had 70,000 members in 1925.[28]

A Triangle of Political Subsystems

To return now to our opening thesis: all these qualifications, however basic, are not in themselves sufficient to undermine the essential value of the East–West dichotomy as an analytic tool. After all, if the tendency to triumphalism, the emphasis on statics rather than dynamics, and the readiness to accept rhetoric as a true reflection of reality are recognized as historically and historiographically endemic to the subject, they can be discounted, neutralized. When the "Western" and "East European" models of Jewish politics are seen not as describing historical facts, empirical processes (*"wie es eigentlich gewesen ist"*), but rather as ideal types that only very rarely, if ever, existed in pure form, they can then be effectively employed as major orientation points essential for the mapping of modern Jewish history.

Thus, at one corner there was the "subworld" of traditional Jewry, often described at the time as a relic of the past, but in fact, as already noted, by no means ineffective in adopting the new to preserve the old. Agudes Yisroel was the most conspicuous example of innovative organization within Orthodox Jewry. The second corner was occupied by what can be called the "Western," but is probably better termed the "emancipationist," type of modern Jewish politics. (The advantage of the term "emancipationist" is that it carries less suggestion of geographical confinement.) Finally, at the third corner was the political subworld called at times "East European" or, alternatively, "the new Jewish politics," but perhaps best named "auto-emancipationist," thus avoiding any suggestion of being place-bound or of monopolizing modern Jewish politics. Examples of emancipationist organizations in more or less unadulterated form were the League of British Jews, established in 1917, and the Centralverein during the period of the Weimar Republic; a classically auto-emancipationist organization was, for instance, the Hibat Zion movement in Russia in the mid-1880s.

Envisaging the development of Jewish politics as a triangle of forces has a number of definite advantages. First, it suggests not a unilinear development in which the new movements and ideologies replaced the old, but rather a growingly complex network of interconnected "subsystems." The politicization of Jewry in modern times involved the multiplication of ideologies and organizations rather than the outright elimination of some by others. This fact is to be explained primarily by the dispersal of Jewry across the world, which was, of course, increasingly reinforced by the mass migrations of the pre-1914 era. Thus, Jewish politics, virtually eliminated by the Communist regime in Soviet Russia, could still continue to develop unhampered in the many independent states across the frontier as well as in the West.

Finally, this particular image carries with it the idea not only of the independence but also of the interdependence of the three "forces." Jewish politics in modern times developed in large part through fundamental ideological strife—the conflict between Orthodoxy and heterodoxy, on the one hand, and the conflict between liberal integrationism and Jewish nationalism, on the other. But the relationship of the three subsystems was not simply one of outright negation. On the contrary, collision produced constant adaptation, adjustment, compromise, coalition. And at least as important was the fact that in the complex unfolding of reality, these forces, in theory so antagonistic, frequently merged to produce new syntheses, hybrid forms, entire areas of overlap that elude simple definition. Here it will suffice, perhaps, to examine two concrete cases in order to illustrate the dialectical nature of the actual historical process.

Complexities and Fluidities: Russian Zionism and the Bund

In many ways the Hibat Zion and the Zionist movement in Russia offer a classic example of "East European" or "auto-emancipationist" politics: a strongly future-oriented program with utopian and quasi-revolutionary implications; nationalist; committed to a program of mass mobilization; hostile to the aspiration of Western Jewry to merge fully (a modified religion apart) into the host nationalities. However, in reality, the development of the proto-Zionist and Zionist movements in Russia depended heavily on links to the West.

It was the idea—or, more accurately, the myth—that Western Jewry would in the last resort provide massive financial help which lent a spurious area of realism to the early faith in Palestinian and territorialist plans, and so permitted the actual formation of the Hibat Zion movement in the 1880s. The same Peretz Smolenskin who rejected the Berlin Haskalah movement with such vehemence still assumed that the Alliance Israélite Universelle would undertake to settle the Jews in Palestine, and was bitterly disappointed when it did not.[29]

On the face of it, of course, the expectations concentrated on the Jewish establishment in the West were absurd. The Alliance and the Conjoint Committee of the Board of Deputies and the Anglo-Jewish Association consistently distanced themselves from Zionism, and some of their most prominent leaders actively opposed—and almost succeeded in sabotaging—the Balfour Declaration in 1917.[30] And yet, however paradoxically, the proto-Zionist and Zionist enterprises were heavily dependent for their survival and ultimate triumph on the West.

The early pioneers in Palestine found work in the agricultural school of the Alliance at Mikveh Israel, and Hibat Zion members such as Eliezer Ben Yehuda were employed in schools established by Western philanthropic organizations or, as in the case of Yehiel Michael Pines, by the Moses Montefiore Fund in Jerusalem. And, of course, the first colonies of the 1880s were only able to survive thanks to the huge amounts of aid from the Baron Edmund de Rothschild in Paris.[31] In 1906, Zangwill's Jewish Territorialist Organization, a breakaway movement from Palestine-centered Zionism, won the support of such prominent members of the American Jewish elite as Oscar Straus[32] and Cyrus L. Sulzberger; and in the critical years 1917–20, the American Jewish Committee under Louis Marshall's leadership took an active part in the campaign to ensure the creation of a national home in Palestine.

There were two very different factors involved here. In some crucial cases, a residual attachment to the ancestral homeland (Eretz Yisrael) provided the bridge between the West and East, between emancipationist and auto-emancipationist. What for the Russian Zionist was part of a radical political strategy could be seen in the West as an act of strictly religious piety (*tsdakah*). Motifs and sentiments rooted in a joint "primordial" tradition, which had lost much of its original force for both sides, still provided some small ground for vitally significant acts of cooperation. The case of Edmund de Rothschild, following in the footsteps of his older relative, Moses Montefiore, is a case in point; the examples of the Mikveh Israel school or the Haifa Technikum were others.

A very different kind of motivation was often also involved, though. As the flow of Jewish immigrants grew from the turn of the century, the "Jewish question" became increasingly internationalized. Fear of an anti-Semitic backlash, of anti-immigration laws, and of a vicious circle of violence and hatred in Eastern Europe if the gates to the West were to close caused real anxiety in the Western Jewish leadership. Territorialist solutions—preferably but not necessarily outside Palestine—thus could be seen as moving from the realm of wild "East European" romanticism and fantasy into that of hard-headed Western realism and even of strict, calculated self-interest. Between the poles of maximalist Zionism and active anti-Zionism stretched a continuum formed by "non-Zionism" in many varieties.

Then again, there was the fact that the Zionist organization established in 1897, unlike the earlier Hibat Zion, was a genuinely international movement with important branches in Germany, England, and the United States. There, the membership, small in normal times, soared during World War I—in America to some 150,000.[33] To a large extent, these recruits were drawn from the immigrant community and the movement was thus something of an East European transplant in the West.

But, there was also a very different category of members—the Western-born and bred. Among them were the leaders of the world movement in the pre-1914 period: Theodor Herzl himself, David Wolfssohn, and Otto Warburg, as well as such key figures as Max Nordau and Louis Dembitz Brandeis. Superficially, this small but remarkably influential group within the movement could be regarded as a somewhat aberrant adjunct to the East European movement (rather as Marxists categorize recruits from the bourgeoisie who choose to join the party of the proletariat).

In fact, though, this type of "postassimilationist Zionism" was very much a sociological phenomenon in its own right.[34] Herzl, Brandeis, and others in this category sought an urgent solution to the Jewish question as *Judennot*—that is, as a socioeconomic and sociopolitical problem—and not to the dilemmas of Judaism in the modern world—a sociopsychological problem. They were alien to Jewish nationalism as understood by Ahad Ha-Am, Ussishkin, and Weizmann, who saw Zionism not only as an answer to anti-Semitism but also as a national revival movement capable of offering the modern Jew a new sense of collective and cultural identity.

In this sense they shared the values characteristic of the Jewish establishment in the West, which was non-Zionist or anti-Zionist. It is, therefore, not surprising that bitter clashes between Russian Zionists and Herzl (and later Herzl's disciples) became so frequent; that the Jewish Territorial Organization founded in 1906 could draw its members from the Zionist as well as the non-Zionist camps in the West; and that eventually in the 1920s Weizmann himself—once Brandeis had felt compelled to leave the movement—became the object of fierce attacks from the Polish Zionists under Yitzhak Gruenbaum, who rejected his plans for closer cooperation with such prominent non-Zionists as Louis Marshall. Thus, if in the post-1945 or post-1948 era, Western Jewry, including even Reform Judaism, has been able to define itself as Zionist, this is due in no small measure to the fact that Zionism in the West has so often been envisaged as a pragmatic, even philanthropic, enterprise rather than as a form of all-embracing nationalism.

The history of the Bund—the General Jewish Labor Union of Lithuania, Russia, and Poland—likewise provides many illustrations of the complex patterns produced by changes of time and place. Committed from 1901 to the idea of Jewish national autonomy within a multinational Russian state; to Yiddish as the national language; to mass revolutionary action against the tsarist autocracy; and to Marxist socialism, it carried all the hallmarks of a classically "East European" or auto-emancipationist movement. And in Eastern Europe, the Bund did act normally as a national revolutionary party. In 1903, it broke away from the Russian Social Democratic Labor Party, which accused it of nationalist separation and of betraying the principles of socialist internationalism. During the 1905 and 1917 revolutions it often acted in de facto union with the other Jewish socialist parties such as the Poale Zion; and in interwar Poland, it cooperated with the left Poale Zion in the Yiddish school movement, Tsisho.

However, in the years 1919–21, as the Bolshevik regime consolidated its hold and the survival of the party in Soviet Russia became impossible, many of the leaders of the Bund (as well as the rank-and-file) chose to throw in their lot with the Communists and joined the Evsektsiia. Of course, the same trend could be observed in the other Jewish socialist parties, but it was significant because it illustrated the inner tension inherent in a movement such as the Bund, which combined Jewish nationalism with would-be orthodox Marxism. Similarly, the Bundist movement in the United States (the Jewish Socialist Federation) frequently deviated from the path usually followed in Eastern Europe. Out of fear that the Zionists were gaining too much influence on the American-Jewish stage, the Jewish Socialist Federation during World War I, like the Jewish Labor Committee in the 1930s, often chose to make common cause with the non-Zionist establishment represented above all by the American Jewish Committee.

Thus, both in Soviet Russia and in the United States it turned out that, in the case of the Bund, too, the barrier dividing the nationalist, auto-emancipationist movements from the forces of anti-nationalism ("assimilationism" in the terminology of the time) was not so solidly impregnable as a strictly ideological analysis might suggest.

Conclusion

To sum up, when every reservation has been stated and every qualification made, care is needed in order not to throw out the baby with the bathwater. At the extremes, the difference between East European (auto-emancipationist) and Western (emancipationist) Jewish politics was really and truly fundamental and of the most dramatic significance.

It could hardly have been otherwise given that the objective circumstances in, let us say, 1881 were so vastly different in the Pale from those prevailing in England, France, or America: On the one hand, a Judeophobic autocracy with its network of discriminatory legislation; a Jewish population of over five million; a demographic explosion; proletarianization and pauperization; mass migration; and a highly traditional community locked in combat with ultramodern, postliberal, anticlerical utopianism. On the other hand, liberal states in which Jews enjoyed all civil rights; Jewish communities still small and secure; economic prosperity; and a gradual erosion of tradition, which encouraged indifferentism and latitudianarianism rather than violent enthusiasms.

Of the very many and important ways (enumerated in part above) in which the gap between the political subsystems found expression, perhaps the most remarkable was the difference in the nature of political involvement. In the West, Jewish political activity, including leadership, was seen in the main as part-time and volunteer, to be supplemented by a paid staff. It was in the Pale that the concept of politics as an all-absorbing commitment caught on. That is why early in the century it became so much the domain of the very young. The full-time organizer, the professional revolutionary, the pioneer—this was a radically new sociological phenomenon in the Jewish community and it was the natural concomitant of ideologies that looked forward to the imminent emergence of a radically new world. It is as though the extremely abrupt transition made by so many from traditional to post-liberal society, from the world of messianic myths to that of secular (or quasi-) "messianism," released extraordinary sources of pent-up energy into politics. Clearly this was a necessary although not an entirely sufficient condition, inter alia, for the creation of the Jewish state in 1948.

Of course, most East European Jews went to America, not to Palestine, but the Yishuv was shaped far more effectively in the image of the post-1881 immigration than was the American Jewish community. Today, American Jewry still sees the synagogue and the temple as the primary cell of the community and its politics in terms of lobbying on behalf of Jewish communities overseas. In Israel the East European radicalism, utopianism, and messianism that, in secular form, made possible the creation of the state, now in various mutations—for ex-

ample, syntheses of nationalism and religious Orthodoxy—still retain
an explosive force.

Notes

1. See, for example, D. Biale, *Power and Powerlessness in Jewish History*
(New York: Schocken, 1986); D.J. Elazar and S.A. Cohen, *The Jewish Polity:
Jewish Political Organization from Biblical Times to the Present* (Bloomington:
Indiana University Press, 1985). Cf. S. Cohen, *The Three Crowns: The Structure
of Communal Politics in Early Rabbinic Jewry* (Cambridge: Cambridge Univer-
sity Press, 1990); C. Goldscheider and A.S. Zuckerman, *The Transformation of
the Jews* (Chicago: University of Chicago Press, 1984).
2. Some of the books published over the last twenty years on the development
of Jewish institutions and politics in the West until 1914 include: M. Lamberti,
Jewish Activism in Imperial Germany: The Struggle for Civil Equality (New
Haven: Yale University Press, 1978); I. Schorsch, *Jewish Reactions to German
Anti-Semitism* (New York: Columbia University Press, 1972); J. Reinharz, *Fa-
therland or Promised Land: The Dilemma of the German Jew 1893–1914* (Ann
Arbor: University of Michigan Press, 1975); P. Albert, *The Modernization of
French Jewry: Consistory and Community in the Nineteenth Century* (Hanover,
NH: Brandeis University Press, 1977); M. Graetz, *Les juifs de France au XIXe
siècle: de la Revolution a la fondation de l'Alliance israélite universelle* (Paris:
Editions de Seuil, 1989); S. Lipman and V.D. Lipman, eds., *The Century of
Moses Montefiore* (Oxford: Oxford University Press, 1982); G.D. Best, *To Free a
People: American Jewish Leaders and the Jewish Problem in Eastern Europe
1890–1914* (Westport, CT: Greenwood, 1982); N.W. Cohen, *Not Free to Desist:
The American Jewish Committee 1906–1966* (Philadelphia: Jewish Publication
Society, 1972).
3. For the more recent historical research on Jewish politics in Eastern Europe
and Palestine before 1914, see, for example, E. Lederhendler, *The Road to Mod-
ern Jewish Politics: Political Tradition and Political Reconstruction in the Jewish
Community of Tsarist Russia* (New York: Oxford University Press, 1989); S.
Laskov, *Ha-biluim* (Tel Aviv: Tel Aviv University, 1979); M. Mishkinsky, *Reshit
tnuat hapoalim ha-yehudit be-rusiya: megamot yesod* (Tel Aviv: Hakibutz Ham-
euhad, 1981); M. Mintz, *Ber Borokhov: ha-maagal ha-rishon (1900–1906)* (Tel
Aviv: Hakibutz Hameuhad, 1976); idem, *Zmanim hadashim, zmirot hadashot:
Ber Borokhov 1914–1917* (Tel Aviv: Am Oved, 1988); idem, *Haver ve-yariv:
Yitshak Tabenkin be-mifleget poale tsiyon 1905–1912* (Tel Aviv: Am Oved,
1986); D. Vital, *The Origins of Zionism* (Oxford: Clarendon Press, 1975); H.J.
Tobias, *The Jewish Bund in Russia: From Its Origins to 1905* (Stanford: Stanford
University Press, 1972); A. Shapira, *Berl. The Biography of a Socialist Zionist:
Berl Katznelson 1887–1944* (Cambridge: Cambridge University Press, 1984); and
the unabridged Hebrew edition, *Berl: biografya*, 2 vols. (Tel Aviv: Am Oved,
1980); S. Tevet, *Kinat David: haye David Ben Gurion*, vol. 1 (Tel Aviv:
Schocken, 1976).
4. [P. Smolenskin], "Am olam," *Ha-shahar III* (1872): pp. 6–16; 73–84; 145–
52; 201–8; 377–84; 433–40; 505–12; 553–66; 643–50; 659–84.

5. M. Hess, *Rom und Jerusalem: die letzte Nationalitätsfrage* (Leipzig: E. Wengler, 1862). Two new biographies of Hess are: S. Avineri, *Moses Hess: Prophet of Communism and Zionism* (New York: New York University Press, 1985); S. Na'aman, *Emanzipation und Messianismus: Leben und Werk des Moses Hess* (Frankfurt am Main: Campus Verlag, 1982).

6. For example, A. Walicki, *The Slavophile Controversy: History of a Conservative Utopia in Nineteenth-Century Russian Thought* (Oxford: Clarendon Press, 1975).

7. E.A. Shils, *Center and Periphery: Essays in Macro-Sociology* (Chicago: University of Chicago Press, 1975).

8. Ahad Ha-Am, "Avdut be-tokh herut," *Kol Kitve Ahad Ha-Am* (Tel-Aviv: Dvir, 1947), pp. 64–69. (First published in *Ha-melits*, February 1891.)

9. On the Central European attitude to the "Ostjuden," see S.E. Aschheim, *Brothers and Strangers: The East European Jew in German and German-Jewish Consciousness* (Madison: University of Wisconsin Press, 1982).

10. On OPE, see I.M. Cherikover [Tcherikower], *Istoriia Obschchestvo dlia rasprostraneniia prosveshcheniia mezhdu evreiami v Rossii* (St. Petersburg: Tipografiia I. Fleitmana, 1913); L.M. Rosental, *Toldot hevrat marbe haskala be-yisrael*, 2 vols. (St. Petersburg: Dfus D.H. Pines, 1885–1890); cf. L. Shapiro, *The History of ORT* (New York: Schocken, 1980).

11. For an analysis of changing leadership patterns among the Russian Jews, see S.J. Zipperstein, "The Politics of Relief: The Transformation of Russian Jewish Communal Life During the First World War," *Studies in Contemporary Jewry*, 4 (1988): 22–40.

12. On the Jewish Social Democratic Party (or ZPS), see H. Grossman, *Der bundizm in galitsye* (Cracow, 1908); and Y. Kisman, "Di yidishe sotsyaldemokratishe bavegung in Galitsye un Bukovine," in G. Aronson et al., eds., *Die geshikhte fun Bund*, vol. 3 (New York: Undzer Tsayt, 1966), pp. 337–482.

13. For example, W. McCagg, *Jewish Nobles and Geniuses in Modern Hungary* (Boulder, CO: East European Monographs, 1972); idem, *A History of Habsburg Jews 1670–1918* (Bloomington: Indiana University Press, 1989), pp. 123–39, 187–97; V. Karady, "Jewish Enrollment Patterns in Classical Secondary Education in Old Regime and Inter-War Hungary," *Studies in Contemporary Jewry*, 1 (1984): 225–52.

14. On the very complicated system used to elect the First and Second Dumas 1906–1907, see H.D. Mehlinger and J.M. Thompson, *Count Witte and the Tsarist Government in the 1905 Revolution* (Bloomington: Indiana University Press, 1972), pp. 241–88; cf. S.S. Harcave, "The Jews and the First Russian National Election," *American and Slavic East European Review*, 9 (1950), no. 1: 33–41; idem, "The Jewish Question in the First Duma," *Jewish Social Studies*, 4 (1944): 155–76.

15. On the religious strand in the development of Hibat Zion and, later, of the Zionist movement, see Y.L. Maimon [Fishman], *Toldot ha-mizrahi* (Jerusalem: Dfus Tsiyon, 1927); E. Luz, *Parallels Meet: Religion and Nationalism in the Early Zionist Movement* (Philadelphia: Jewish Publication Society, 1988); G. Bat-Yehuda, *Ish ha-meorot: Yitshak Yaakov Reines* (Jerusalem: Mossad Harav Kook, 1985); Y. Elichai, "Tnuat ha-mizrahi be-polin ha-kongresait 1916–1927" (doctoral dissertation, The Hebrew University of Jerusalem, 1988).

16. G.C. Bacon, "Agudath Israel in Poland 1916–1939: An Orthodox Jewish Response to the Challenge of Modernity" (doctoral dissertation, Columbia University, New York, 1979).

17. E. Mendelsohn, *The Jews of East Central Europe Between the World Wars* (Bloomington: Indiana University Press, 1983), p. 66.

18. Idem, *Zionism in Poland: The Formative Years, 1915–1926* (New Haven: Yale University Press, 1981), p. 108.

19. Y. Slutsky, *Ha-itonut ha-yehudit-rusit be-reshit ha-mea ha-esrim 1900–1918* (Tel Aviv: Ha-makhon le-heker ha-tfutsot, 1978), pp. 17–18; Y. Maor, *Sheelat ha-yehudim ba-tnua ha-liberalit ve-hamehapahnit be-rusya 1890–1914* (Jerusalem: Mossad Bialik, 1964), p. 48.

20. The attraction exerted by revolutionary internationalism on a relatively high number of Jews is discussed, inter alia, in: I. Deutscher, *The Non-Jewish Jew and Other Essays* (London: Oxford University Press, 1968); J.L. Talmon, *The Myth of the Nation and the Vision of Revolution: The Origins of Ideological Polarization in the Twentieth Century* (London: Secker and Warburg, 1981); J.M. Cuddihy, *The Ordeal of Civility: Freud, Marx, Levi-Strauss and the Jewish Struggle with Modernity* (New York: Basic Books, 1974); M. Löwy, *Rédemption et utopie: le judaïsme libertaire en Europe centrale; une étude d'affinité elective* (Paris, 1988).

21. Zvi Gitelman, *Jewish Nationality and Soviet Politics: The Jewish Sections of the CPSU 1917–1930* (Princeton: Princeton University Press, 1972); M. Altschuler, *Ha-yevsektsia be-vrit ha-moetsot (1981–1930): ben leumiut le-komunizm* (Jerusalem: Moreshet and Sifriat Hapoalim, 1980).

22. On the participation of Jews in the Polish Communist movement, see S. Zakharyash, *Di komunistishe bavegung tsvishn der yidisher arbetendiker bafelkerung in poyln* (Warsaw: Yidish Bukh, 1954); P. Mints, *Di geshikhte fun a falsher iluzye: zikhroynes* (Buenos Aires: Yidbukh, 1954).

23. Mendelsohn, *The Jews of East Central Europe*, p. 77. Cf. I. Oppenheim, *Tnuat he-haluts be-polin: 1917–1929* (Jerusalem: Magnes Press, 1982).

24. For example, H.J. Tobias with C.E. Woodhouse, eds., "Political Reaction and Revolutionary Careers: The Jewish Bundists in Defeat 1907–1910," *Comparative Studies in History and Society*, 19 (1977): 367–96.

25. Mendelsohn, *Zionism in Poland*, p. 184.

26. Idem, *The Jews of East Central Europe*, pp. 77–78.

27. Y.S. Hertz, "Der Bund in umophengikn poyln," (i) "1918–1925" in S. Dubnov-Ehrlich et al., eds., *Di geshikhte fun Bund,* vol. 4 (New York: Undzer Tsayt, 1972), pp. 9–77; (ii) "1926–1932," ibid., vol. 5 (New York: Undzer Tsayt, 1981), pp. 9–144; B.K. Johnpoll, *The Politics of Futility: The General Jewish Worker Bund of Poland 1917–1943* (Ithaca: Cornell University Press, 1967); J. Marcus, *Social and Political History of the Jews in Poland, 1919–1939* (Berlin: Mouton, 1983), p. 283.

28. Reinharz, *Fatherland or Promised Land*, pp. 52–53.

29. P. Smolenskin, "Derekh laavor geulim," *Ha-shahar*, 10 (1879–82): 329–56; "Harimu mikhshol mi-derekh ami," ibid., 11 (1882–83): 73–83.

30. The literature on the events leading up to the Balfour Declaration is by now most extensive. See, for example, L. Stein, *The Balfour Declaration* (London: Valentine Mitchell, 1961); I. Friedman, *The Question of Palestine, 1914–*

1918: British-Jewish-Arab Relations (London: Routledge and Kegan Paul, 1973), R. Sanders, *The High Walls of Jerusalem: A History of the Balfour Declaration and the Birth of the British Mandate for Palestine* (New York: Henry Holt, 1983); D. Vital, *Zionism: The Crucial Phase* (Oxford: Clarendon Press, 1987).

31. For example, S. Schama, *Two Rothschilds and the Land of Israel* (London: Collins, 1978); D. Giladi, "Ha-baron, ha-pkidut ve-hamoshavot ha-rishonot be-erets yisrael: haarkha me-hadash," *Cathedra*, 2 (1976): 59–68.

32. See N. Cohen, *A Dual Heritage: The Public Career of Oscar S. Straus* (Philadelphia: Jewish Publication Society, 1972).

33. E. Friesel, "The Influence of American Zionism on the American Jewish Community, 1900–1950," *American Jewish History*, 75 (1985–86): 141.

34. The concept of "postassimilation" Zionism is attributed to Kurt Blumenfeld; see, for example, S.M. Poppel, *Zionism in Germany 1897–1933: The Shaping of a Jewish Identity* (Philadelphia: Jewish Publication Society, 1977), pp. 46–50.

Was There a "Jewish Politics" in Western and Central Europe?

PAULA E. HYMAN

The nascent field of Jewish political history has laid to rest the myth that Jews had no political history until the end of the nineteenth century. Rejecting the notion that territory and sovereignty were prerequisites for the exercise of political power, historians and political scientists have explored the nature of Jewish political theory and practice throughout history. They have uncovered a rich and diverse tradition, which was reflected both in the internal governance of the autonomous Jewish community and in its relations with external political institutions, whether ecclesiastical or secular. And they have argued that, despite their vulnerability as a despised minority, Jews displayed considerable political skill in attaining a modicum of security within a frequently hostile larger society.[1]

When turning their attention to the development of Jewish politics in the modern period, historians and political scientists have focused, not surprisingly, on those areas where Jewish populations formed specifically Jewish political parties and engaged openly in the political process as Jews—that is, on the countries of East Central Europe and Eastern Europe as well as their immigrant daughter communities, primarily in the New World. They have also explored the ideology and implementation of Zionism, the most important Jewish political movement of the modern era. However, they have devoted scant attention to the emancipated Jewish communities of Western and Central Europe, or rather have limited their attention to the questions of emancipation and self-defense. This is understandable, for the Jews of Western and Central Europe lacked both the numbers and the ethnic self-consciousness so crucial to the formation of Jewish political parties.[2]

In defining Jewish politics in Western and Central Europe as a matter of struggling for emancipation and then defending Jewish rights against the onslaught of anti-Semitism, students of Western and Central European Jewish communities have implicitly accepted the terms in which these communities presented themselves to the larger society. The emancipation debate—which extended from the last third of the eighteenth century until 1870—made it clear that Jews were granted rights as individuals and that the organized Jewish community had no legitimate political interests beyond the defense of freedom of religion. Throughout Western and Central Europe articulate Jews of all religious tendencies accepted this premise and based their public statements upon it; they shunned partisan politics as Jews.[3] Yet, as recent studies of the processes of emancipation and assimilation have demonstrated, the image of an apolitical emancipated Jewish community, in thrall to its assimilationist goals, hardly does justice to the diverse political activism of emancipated European Jewries. During the period of the struggle for emancipation and thereafter, the organized Jewish communities of England, France, Germany, and Austria lobbied vigorously for the enforcement of the civic rights and freedom of religious expression which its members, like all other citizens, enjoyed by law and entered the realm of international politics to defend their persecuted brethren in the Levant and Eastern Europe. In fact, the particular nature of the struggle for emancipation and later for defense of Jewish rights shaped the political socialization and mobilization of each country's Jewish population. In choosing to defend their own rights as citizens or potential citizens, European Jews developed a general political stance.[4]

Given the public political activity of the emancipated Jewish communities of the West, within the limits set by the terms of emancipation, it is worthwhile to extend our inquiry to explore the collective, though often unacknowledged, political behavior of Jews in Western and Central Europe that lies beyond those limits. In doing so, we can bring a broader perspective to the study of the politics of European Jewry, which has been dominated by the East European Jewish experience. The study of the politics of emancipated Jewish communities of the West illustrates the importance of local factors—both within the political culture of the host country as well as within the Jewish communities themselves—in determining the political activity of Jewish populations.

The study of modern Jewish politics in Eastern Europe and the United States takes as a given a liberal or left-of-center pattern of Jewish political behavior which distinguishes the Jews from their fellow countrymen. The central scholarly debate concerns the sources of Jewish political distinctiveness. One school of thought argues, broadly speaking, for a "situational" understanding of Jewish politics; the other for a cultural influence. According to the first, the disproportionate representation of East European Jews in left-of-center and radical politics stems from several factors. Their experience of discrimination and the realization of their blocked mobility reduces the stake of both Jewish students and artisans in the ruling political system. Particularly in the Russian Empire, where they are receptive to the ideologies of the Russian revolutionary movements, the politically active elements in the Jewish community opt for a radical restructuring of polity and society as the best means to secure civic equality, economic opportunity, and "social justice." On a more abstract level, they recognize that only within a new social order, in which Jews would participate from the outset in shaping both values and institutions, would they achieve true equality. In polities that looked back to the Christian Middle Ages for their myths, Jews would remain forever alien or, at best, marginal.[5] According to the cultural school, situational factors, though important, are insufficient to account for the predilection of modern Jews for liberal and radical politics. Rather, elements within traditional Jewish culture, in particular, its concern for the realization of social justice in the here and now as well as its messianism, *when secularized*, predispose Jews toward liberalism, anarchism, or socialism. Some have even argued for similarities in deep structure, in pattern of thought, between traditional Jewish doctrine and some forms of radicalism.[6]

In their political behavior the emancipated Jews of Western and Central Europe demonstrate the primacy of situational factors in determining patterns of Jewish political mobilization. Until their emancipation was secured (at different times in the eighteenth and nineteenth centuries), Jews in England, France, Germany, and Austria followed the model of a traditional Jewish politics, which was generally favorable toward the established order. This is not surprising, since the ruling prince, whether secular or ecclesiastical, conferred privileges of settlement and offered protection for "his Jews." Only after Jews were enfranchised did they begin to develop a range of political stances—a truly modern politics—within the constellation of European nation-states. As with all groups, Jewish political activism emerged first among the economic and intellectual elite, spreading to the masses only with the acceptance of universal male suffrage. Because political activism was not characteristic of the Jewish community as a whole, generalizations about the politics of French or German Jewry are based upon public statements of Jewish leadership, articles in the Jewish press, and the assessments of contemporaries.[7]

The varieties of Jewish political behavior manifested in Western and Central Europe in the nineteenth and twentieth centuries depended largely upon the difficulty of the battle for emancipation and upon the degree of acceptance of emancipation within the larger society. Where there prevailed a broad consensus about the nature of the state, which included Jews as a matter of course, Jews could be found among the supporters of a number of political parties. Socioeconomic status and Jewish denominational affiliation would play a large part in determining political choices. Where the consensus about the admissibility of Jews within civil society was a narrow one, and where that consensus became increasingly restricted, Jews supported the party or parties— generally liberal, and, in the twentieth century, socialist—that they perceived as most likely to defend the vision of state and society essential for Jewish equality and for the success of individual Jews.

To be sure, the most prominent Jewish political figures, both activists and ideologues, in Western and Central Europe—with the notable exception of Benjamin Disraeli—were associated with radicalism. As early as 1848 German artisans in Leipzig proclaimed their antipathy toward those Jewish intellectuals, like Karl Marx and Ferdinand Lassalle, who fomented revolution. Within the ranks of these early Jewish socialists in Germany was Moses Hess, whose *Rome and Jerusalem* (1862) was the first statement of a modern secular Zionism. By the end of the century Eduard Bernstein had emerged as the leader of the Social Democratic Party in Germany, Léon Blum had embarked upon the political career that would bring him in 1936 to the position of France's first Socialist (and first Jewish) premier, and Bernard Lazare had attracted public attention as a radical intellectual and vigorous champion of Alfred Dreyfus. At the conclusion of World War I, Jews also played a highly visible role in German radical politics. Four of the eleven members of the central committee of the newly formed German Communist Party were Jews. In the short-lived revolutions that erupted in Berlin and Munich in 1918–19 such Jewish activists as Rosa Luxemburg, Kurt Eisner, Gustav Landauer, and Ernst Toller, among others, emerged as central leaders.[8]

Like their counterparts among the revolutionary Jewish leaders of East Central and Eastern Europe, these Western Jewish radical intellectuals were influenced, at least in part, by their marginality as acculturated Jews. Living within European societies that persisted in labeling even converts as Jews and whose secular symbols derived from their Christian past, they were alienated from ideas that reinforced the traditional social order and attracted to critiques that provided a universalist basis for social organization. Unlike their counterparts in the East, they lacked both a Jewish constituency and a multiethnic environment implicitly supportive of ethnic politics. Until the arrival of Jewish immigrants from Eastern Europe, there was no Jewish working class to speak of in the West (though there were poor Jews). Although they attracted considerable attention and were always, much to their distress, publicly perceived and discussed as Jews, Jewish radicals in Western and Central Europe did not function within a Jewish social context. Nor did they represent a significant trend among the Jews of their countries, who were, by and large, loyal to liberalism as long as they could be.

In committing their energy and financial support to liberalism in Western and Central Europe, Jews contributed to the formulation of a vision of a pluralistic constitutional democracy as the basis for the modern nation-state. Even as they denied the existence of a specific "Jewish politics," Western and Central European Jews as a group became the most consistent supporters of the *Rechtsstaat*, the state based upon constitutional law rather than common ethnic or religious heritage. In their self-defense efforts they challenged the notion that popular prejudice—empowered in the expression of the popular will through universal suffrage—could override the law. To illustrate these generalizations, I will draw examples from the participation of Jews in French, German, Austrian, and British politics in the nineteenth and early twentieth centuries.

France

As the first Jews to be emancipated, the Jews of France knew full well that they owed their civic equality to the triumph of the revolution. Yet, the French experience permitted a diversity of political affiliations for French Jewry. Although emancipation was the direct result of the revolution, the revolution's legacy was mixed. Anti-Jewish riots in 1789, 1830, and 1848, as well as Napoleon I's discriminatory decrees, were also phenomena linked to revolutionary ferment. Moreover, a succession of regimes throughout the nineteenth century—Bourbon and Orléanist royalist, Napoleonic imperial, and republican—ratified, and extended, the equality of Jews as citizens. Thus, for example, a Bourbon government allowed Napoleon's discriminatory anti-Jewish decrees to lapse; governmental subsidy of the costs of the Jewish religious establishment and of Jewish primary schools as well as the abolition of the oath *more judaico* occurred during the Orléanist July Monarchy; the postrevolutionary government of 1848–49 opened two ministries for the first time to nonconverted Jews; the Emperor Napoleon III maintained cordial relations with the organized Jewish community; and a republican government in 1870 extended French citizenship to Jews living in Algeria.[9]

The acceptance across much of the political spectrum of the right of Jews to equality enabled French Jews to choose their political affiliations based upon factors other than their Jewish origins. While the professionals who founded the Alliance Israélite Universelle in 1860 were convinced republicans, the patrician James de Rothschild, like many of his class, was a legitimist. And French Jewish leaders repeatedly heralded the political neutrality of their community.[10]

For the majority of French Jews, however, their middle-class status as well as the association of the Bourbon legitimists with a vision of France based upon the Catholic Church, a precapitalist economy, and France's medieval tradition, rather than upon *liberté, egalité, and fraternité*, effectively eliminated the Right as a political option. Indeed, the most visible and threatening manifestations of anti-Semitism in nineteenth-century France emanated from the political Right.[11]

With the emergence of the Third Republic in the last quarter of the nineteenth century, French Jews became ardent supporters of a liberal republicanism which drew its symbols from France's revolutionary tradition.[12] As one French Jewish journal, the *Archives israélites*, declared upon the centenary of the revolution in 1889, "[L]iberalism, the scrupulous respect for beliefs, the sincere and honest guarantee of the sacred rights of conscience, *voilà l'ami*."[13] Where the organized Jewish community deviated from French republicanism was in the Jewish repudiation of anticlericalism. True, French Jews identified a triumphalist Catholic Church as dangerous to their interests, and several prominent French anticlericals were Jews.[14] However, as a religious community, French Jewry recognized that radical republican anticlericalism undermined their own claim to a particularist identity within the French nation as well as to governmental support and recognition of their communal institutions.[15] Indeed, French Jewish spokesmen sought "the triumph of the spirit of moderation and the spirit of pacification in politico-religious matters."[16] While their numbers were never significant enough to influence the course of republican politics in France, Jews did give expression to a republicanism that was pluralist and religiously tolerant even as it embraced the centrality of revolutionary ideals for France's national identity.

England

In England as in France, Jews had available a number of political options. Despite the fact that the Liberal Party had campaigned for Jewish emancipation throughout the middle years of the nineteenth century while notions of "the Christian state" were still being articulated among the Tories, many of the Anglo-Jewish elite proclaimed Tory sympathies and urged their fellow Jews to vote for that party. The London *Jewish Chronicle* even took great pride in the distribution of Jewish votes across the political spectrum. In 1885 it crowed, "Surprise or no surprise, Jews actually do support Radicals; wonder or no wonder, Jews are often Tory. The fact is that Jews have become so thoroughly English that they regard their responsibility as voters entirely as Englishmen."[17] In areas of Jewish residential concentration the Jewish vote was even courted by both sides.[18]

The growing acceptance, by Tories as well as Liberals, of the civic integration of Jews might have fostered a further "normalization" of Jewish voting patterns, had it not been for the Tories' promotion of anti-alienism in the last decades of the nineteenth century and the beginning of the twentieth. Although the anti-alien campaign avoided statements of overt anti-Semitism, the immigrants who were labeled as undesirable were East European Jews. Anglo-Jews, along with Jewish citizens of immigrant origins, felt that their own status was demeaned by the disparagement of the new immigrant Jew, by the failure to recognize that the Jewish immigrant had the potential to become a valuable and loyal Englishman. After 1904, when the first Aliens Bill was introduced, Jews voted heavily for Liberal candidates and the *Jewish Chronicle* abandoned its traditional nonpartisan stance. Thus, specific issues that were seen as casting aspersions on Jewish civic status in general, could become determining factors in Jewish political mobilization.[19]

The German Lands and Austria

In countries where nationalist movements increasingly promoted the notion of full equality only for those sharing the historical national origin of their land, Jews did not have the luxury of distributing themselves as far across the political spectrum as they did in France or England. In the German states, where the emancipation debate was bitter and prolonged, Jews, with the exception of a small number of political activists, cast their lot with the liberals—but only when and where the liberals seemed capable of delivering civic equality. Thus, before the revolution of 1848, when the liberals were split in their attitudes toward Jewish emancipation, and in the period of reaction following the defeat of the revolution, the masses of German Jews appear to have opted for political loyalism. The convergence of their own embourgeoisement and the growing power of liberalism within Germany after 1860 enabled Jews to find in liberal politics support for both their economic and their Jewish political interests.[20]

By the end of the nineteenth century and the beginning of the twentieth, however, the match of class and religio-ethnic interests increasingly diverged for the Jews of Germany and Austria. As they became committed to defending their civil rights in a political fashion, they were compelled to move leftward (in Germany, first to the Progressives and later to the Social Democrats) as the mainstream liberal parties, bowing to the popularity of anti-Semitism, became ever more lukewarm in their public defense of Jewish equality.[21] In Weimar Germany the major defense organization of German Jewry, the Centralverein, collaborated closely, though discreetly, with the Social Democrats to defend Jewish rights by buttressing German democracy. Many German Jews also cast their votes for the party, despite their distaste for its socialist economic policies.[22] Similarly, in interwar Vienna, the majority of Jews voted for the Austrian Social Democratic Party. As George Clare (Klaar), the son of an assimilated middle-class family, recounts in his memoirs, "We were, of course, all Social-Democrats. What other party could a Jew vote for? The Social-Democrats were, at least offic-ially, not anti-Semitic, and many of their leaders were Jews." Yet Clare emphasized his family's lack of enthusiasm for the party. "Most of the Klaars were merely Social Democratic voters. Their socialist convic-tions could easily have been knocked down with the feather of liberal-ism, had a worthwhile Liberal Party still been in existence."[23]

Even as their voting patterns moved leftward, Jews proved to be the most articulate defenders of a nonethnocentric democratic liberalism. Indeed, some Jewish liberals argued that their form of all-inclusive liberalism was the best model for the nation-state. Thus, one Austrian Jewish liberal went so far as to state in 1907, when nationalist politics dominated within Austria, "Yes, I would like to believe that ... we Jews in Austria are above all the best Austrians. While the nationalists, Slavs, or Germans only want a national [Austria], the clericalists, only a clerical [Austria], the feudalists, only a feudal [Austria], the Social-ists a Socialist Austria, we Jews want an Austria *sans phrase*." [24]

Conclusion

If there was a distinctive Jewish political style in Western and Central Europe, it lay in this promotion of a pluralistic liberalism. Western and Central European Jews adhered to, and publicized, a liberalism that depicted the state as a rational construct embracing all those who de-clared their loyalty as citizens. It was precisely this rational Jewish patriotism that the nationalist intellectual Maurice Barrès derided: "The Jews do not have a country in the sense that we understand it. For us, *la patrie* is our soil and our ancestors, the land of our dead. For them, it is the place where their self-interest is best pursued. Their intellectuals thus arrive at their famous definition. '*La patrie*, it is an idea!' But which idea? That which is most useful for them—for exam-ple, the idea that all men are brothers, that nationality is a prejudice to be destroyed."[25] While Barrès clearly disapproved of the concept of the nation that Western Jews held, it is not evident that he completely distorted that concept. Moreover, elsewhere, he acknowledged the vigor of Jewish patriotism, even if its source was intellectual rather than instinctual.[26]

Although the ideal of the liberal state was not a Jewish invention, it did serve the interests of Jews seeking civic and social integration as well as economic mobility. For reasons of the national culture of the host countries as well as the predilections of the Jews themselves, a Diaspora nationalist self-concept and politics were not viable in the West. The tragedy for Western and Central European Jews, then, lay in the fragility of liberal ideals within their societies. By the turn of the century, the Jewish champions of liberalism, particularly in Germany and Austria, found themselves with few political allies. Even ostensibly liberal parties sought to distance themselves from identification with the Jews. Where once the issue of Jewish emancipation had been a touchstone for liberalism, now the defense of "Jewish interests" was a political liability. Yet Western and Central European Jews of the middle classes had no viable political address other than liberalism. Where liberalism failed, European Jews became politically irrelevant.

Notes

1. For an important first statement of the theme of Jewish political sagacity, see Ismar Schorsch, "On the History of the Political Judgment of the Jew," Leo Baeck Memorial Lecture no. 20 (New York, 1976). For pioneering work in the field of Jewish political theory, see Daniel J. Elazar and Stuart A. Cohen, *The Jewish Polity* (Bloomington: Indiana University Press, 1985); and the essays in Daniel J. Elazar, ed., *Kinship and Consent: The Jewish Political Tradition and Its Contemporary Uses* (Washington, DC: University Press of America, 1983). For a general, popularized summation of the new approach to Jewish political studies, see David Biale, *Power and Powerlessness in Jewish History* (New York: Schocken Books, 1986).

2. For an example of the lack of attention paid to the politics of West European Jews, see Biale, *Power and Powerlessness*, pp. 118, 124–25. On the Jewish political struggle to achieve and safeguard the gains of emancipation, see Jacob Katz, *Out of the Ghetto* (Cambridge: Harvard University Press, 1973); M.C.N. Salbstein, *The Emancipation of the Jews in Britain* (Rutherford, Madison, and Teaneck, NJ: Fairleigh Dickinson University Press, 1982); Phyllis Cohen Albert, *The Modernization of French Jewry* (Hanover, NH: Brandeis University Press, 1977), and Robert Liberles, "Was There a Jewish Movement for Emancipation in Germany?" *Leo Baeck Institute Yearbook*, 31 (1986), pp. 35–49. On Jewish self-defense efforts in Europe, see Ismar Schorsch, *Jewish Reactions to German Antisemitism, 1870–1914* (New York: Columbia University Press, 1972); Jehudah Reinharz, *Fatherland or Promised Land* (Ann Arbor: University of Michigan Press, 1975); Marjorie Lamberti, *Jewish Activism in Imperial Germany* (New Haven and London: Yale University Press, 1978); Mikhael Graetz, *Haperiferya hay'ta l'merkaz* (Jerusalem: Mosad Bialik, 1982), pp. 281–322; Phyllis Albert, *The Modernization of French Jewry*, pp. 151–69; Marsha L. Rozenblit, *The Jews of Vienna, 1867–1914* (Albany: SUNY Press, 1983), pp. 175–93. For a comprehensive study of radical Jewish politics in prerevolutionary Russia, see Jonathan Frankel, *Prophecy and Politics* (Cambridge and New York: Cambridge Univer-

sity Press, 1981). On Jewish politics in interwar Poland and in the Soviet Union, see Ezra Mendelsohn, "The Dilemma of Jewish Politics in Poland: Four Responses," in George Mosse and Bela Vago, eds., *Jews and Non-Jews in Eastern Europe* (New York: Wiley, 1974), pp. 203–20; and Zvi Gitelman, *Jewish Nationality and Soviet Politics* (Princeton: Princeton University Press, 1972). The literature on Zionism is too voluminous to cite. For a general history in English, see Walter Laqueur, *A History of Zionism* (New York: Holt, Rinehart and Winston, 1972). For the political development of Zionism in a major community, see Ezra Mendelsohn, *Zionism in Poland: The Formative Years, 1915–1926* (New Haven and London: Yale University Press, 1981). For the communal impact of the political struggle of Zionists and their opponents, see Stuart A. Cohen, *English Zionists and British Jews* (Princeton: Princeton University Press, 1982).

3. On the emancipation debate, see Katz, *Out of the Ghetto*, pp. 57–103; and Arthur Hertzberg, *The French Enlightenment and the Jews* (New York: Columbia University Press, 1968). On the political stance of emancipated Jews, see Michael Marrus, *The Politics of Assimilation* (New York: Oxford University Press, 1971), pp. 86–121; Paula Hyman, *From Dreyfus to Vichy* (New York: Columbia University Press, 1979), pp. 8–11; and Jacob Toury, *Die politische Orientierungen der Juden in Deutschland* (Tübingen: J.C.B. Mohr, 1966).

4. In addition to the works of Schorsch, Lamberti, Albert, Graetz, and Hyman cited above, see Carol Iancu, *Les Juifs de Roumanie 1866–1919* (Aix-en-Provence: Editions de l'Université de Provence, 1978); and Michael Laskier, *The Alliance Israélite Universelle and the Jewish Communities of Morocco 1862–1962* (Albany: SUNY Press, 1983), pp. 31–95. Lamberti, in particular, points out that defense against anti-Semitism stimulated what she has called "the breakthrough to political activism." See her *Jewish Activism*, pp. 7–13.

5. For effective presentations of the "situational" argument, see Robert Brym, *The Jewish Intelligentsia and Russian Marxism* (New York: Schocken Books, 1978); Robert Wistrich, *Revolutionary Jews from Marx to Trotsky* (New York: Barnes and Noble Books, 1976); John Murray Cuddihy, *The Ordeal of Civility* (New York: Basic Books, 1974), pp. 135–50; Calvin Goldscheider and Alan S. Zuckerman, *The Transformation of the Jews* (Chicago: University of Chicago Press, 1984), pp. 116–20; Isaac Deutscher, "The Non-Jewish Jew," in *The Non-Jewish Jew and Other Essays* (London: Oxford University Press, 1968), pp. 25–41; and Jacob Talmon, "Jews Between Revolution and Counter-Revolution," *Israel Among the Nations* (London: Weidenfeld and Nicolson, 1970), pp. 1–87. While Talmon emphasizes the impact of Enlightenment and emancipation upon Jewish self-consciousness in the modern period, he also points to "the ancient messianic disposition" as the absorber of the feelings of dislocation experienced by Jews in the modern world.

6. For the most recent statement of the cultural position, see Gerald Sorin, *The Prophetic Minority* (Bloomington: Indiana University Press, 1985). For a structural anthropological argument about the homology of traditional Judaism and anarchism, see Michael Löwy, "Jewish Messianism and Libertarian Utopia in Central Europe (1900–1933)," *New German Critique*, Special Issue no. 2: Germans and Jews (Spring–Summer 1980): 105–15.

7. For an analysis of the traditional politics of medieval Jewry, see Schorsch, "On the History," pp. 8–12; and Biale, *Power and Powerlessness*, pp. 58–83. Be-

cause it is so difficult to ascertain the political ideology of the Jewish masses, especially before the introduction of universal suffrage, statistical tables of Jewish political preferences in the nineteenth century (as in Jacob Toury's pioneering *Die politische Orientierungen*) are not trustworthy.

8. On Marx, Lassalle, Bernstein, Lazare, Blum, and Luxemburg, see the biographical studies in Wistrich, *Revolutionary Jews*. For Moses Hess, see Shlomo Avineri, *The Making of Modern Zionism* (New York: Basic Books, 1981), pp. 36–46. On the Jewish role in the postwar German revolutions, see Jerry Z. Muller, "Communism, Anti-Semitism, and the Jews," *Commentary* (August 1988): 30–31.

9. On nineteenth-century French Jewish history, see Patrick Girard, *Les Juifs de France de 1789 à 1860* (Paris: Calmann-Lévy, 1976); François Delpech, "La Révolution et l'Empire," and "De 1815 à 1894" in Bernhard Blumenkranz, ed., *Histoire des juifs de France* (Toulouse: Privat, 1972), pp. 265–346; Albert, *The Modernization of French Jewry*, pp. 122–69.

10. Girard, *Les Juifs*, pp. 160–63; Marrus, *The Politics of Assimilation*, pp. 122–24.

11. Stephen Wilson, *Ideology and Experience: Antisemitism in France at the Time of the Dreyfus Affair* (Rutherford, Madison, and Teaneck, NJ: Fairleigh Dickinson University Press, 1982), pp. 613–18; Marrus, *The Politics of Assimilation*, pp. 124–25. Although the French Left, both socialist and anarchist, indulged in anti-Semitic rhetoric and iconography as an aspect of its anticapitalism, by the time of the Dreyfus Affair the most powerful anti-Semitism in France was located on the political Right. For the anti-Semitic iconography of the Affair see Norman L. Kleeblatt, ed., *The Dreyfus Affair: Art, Truth, and Justice* (Berkeley: University of California Press, 1987).

12. Marrus, *The Politics of Assimilation*, pp. 126–27.

13. *Archives israélites*, 3 October 1889, pp. 317–18, as cited in Marrus, *The Politics of Assimilation*, p. 134.

14. *Archives israélites*, 9 July 1885, p. 217; 1 June 1886, p. 568; 15 March 1888, p. 82; Marrus, *The Politics of Assimilation*, pp. 128–31.

15. Marrus, *The Politics of Assimilation*, p. 131; Hyman, *From Dreyfus to Vichy*, p. 10.

16. *Archives israélites*, 3 October 1889, p. 318, as cited in Marrus, *The Politics of Assimilation*, p. 135.

17. *Jewish Chronicle*, 26 November 1885, p. 9, as cited in John A. Garrard, *The English and Immigration 1880–1910* (London and New York: Oxford University Press, 1971), p. 116.

18. Ibid., pp. 119.

19. Ibid., pp. 33–34, 38–40, 120–31.

20. Toury, *Die politische Orientierungen*, pp. 16–28; and Heinz Holeczek, "The Jews and the German Liberals," *Leo Baeck Institute Yearbook*, 28 (1983): 77–91. This situation illustrates Peter Medding's claim that Jews have an overarching interest in political stability, as long as the regime permits the free exercise of Judaism and the pursuit of economic survival. See his "Toward a General Theory of Jewish Political Interests and Behavior," in Elazar, ed., *Kinship and Consent*, pp. 313–43. On the link between Jewish emancipation and the general trends of industrialization and embourgeoisement in Germany, see Reinhard

Rürup, "Jewish Emancipation and Bourgeois Society," *Leo Baeck Institute Yearbook*, 14 (1969): 67–91; and his "German Liberalism and the Emancipation of the Jews," *Leo Baeck Institute Yearbook*, 20 (1975): 59–68.

21. For discussion of the shift to the Progressives, see Lamberti, *Jewish Activism*, pp. 23–54; and her "Liberals, Socialists and the Defence against Antisemitism in the Wilhelmian Period," *Leo Baeck Institute Yearbook*, 25 (1980): 147–62. In opposition to Toury's critique of Jewish leadership, Lamberti sees the alliance with the Progressives as the only realistic alternative for German Jewry.

22. For Jewish support of the Social Democratic Party in Weimar Germany, see Donald Niewyk, *Socialist, Anti-Semite, and Jew* (Baton Rouge: Louisiana State University Press, 1971), pp. 58–59, 190, 216; and idem, *The Jews in Weimar Germany* (Baton Rouge: Louisiana State University Press, 1980), pp. 25–30. Niewyk argues that Jewish electoral support for the SPD became significant only after 1930 and that many bourgeois Jews could not bring themselves to support the party because of its class-conscious rhetoric.

23. George Clare, *Last Waltz in Vienna: The Rise and Destruction of a Family, 1842–1942* (New York: Holt, Rinehart and Winston, 1982), p. 105. (I would like to thank Harriet Freidenreich for bringing this passage to my attention.)

24. As cited in Rozenblit, *The Jews of Vienna*, p. 183.

25. Maurice Barrès, *Scènes et doctrines du nationalisme*, I (Paris: Librairie Plon, 1925), pp. 67–68. The book was first published in 1902.

26. Maurice Barrès, *Les diverses familles spirituelles de la France* (Paris: Emil-Paul frères, 1917), p. 67.

The "New Jewish Politics" in the United States

Historical Perspectives

PETER Y. MEDDING

To appreciate what is distinctive about the contemporary politics of American Jews (as well as what it has in common with the political behavior of Jews in other times and other places), we begin with an analysis of different patterns of Jewish politics. These are broad models—theoretical approximations combining the essential elements of these patterns—that serve as measuring rods for understanding and comparing diverse and complex particular historical situations. While three such patterns are identified, and discussed here—traditional Jewish politics; modern Jewish politics; and the new Jewish politics—the greater part of the chapter is devoted to the last of these.

Patterns of Jewish Politics

The characteristic pattern of politics of the corporate Jewish communities in Europe from the medieval period until emancipation—traditional Jewish politics—never existed in the United States. Commonly referred to as *shtadlanut* (intercession), traditional Jewish politics consisted in the main of personal intercession on behalf of the corporate community by individual Jews who had access to the authorities, often arising out of the latter's economic needs or dependence. These intercessors utilized their elite connections or influence to plead for the Jews—entreating, requesting, persuading (and sometimes bribing) rulers to grant them residence permits, protection, toleration, or to reduce taxes, but always *as a matter of grace or favor*. In return, the Jews would show their gratitude in various ways.[1]

The key elements of traditional Jewish politics were a Jewish political status that was devoid of rights, had constantly to be renegotiated, and was therefore fundamentally insecure and permanently vulnerable; a strategy of political action that relied upon personal, behind-the-scenes influence; and the hope or expectation of acquiring a grant of favor or grace (and the fear and reality of expulsion, increased taxation, and other sanctions) if the intercession failed.

Emancipation gave rise to a new pattern. While most developed in democratic societies, modern Jewish politics was not confined to them. It involved the pursuit by Jews of the benefits of citizenship, and where present, of liberty and equality as a matter of *right*, and for the removal of impediments to their enjoyment of those benefits—particularly those arising from prejudice and discrimination and from restrictions upon the maintenance of Judaism, Jewish cultural life, and communal institutions. Such claims were generally pressed by the leaders of Jewish organizations. This reflected the political mobilization of the Jewish mass public in the pursuit of Jewish political concerns, a process that was further promoted by the development of a Jewish press.[2] Although resort was sometimes made to personal, nonpublic representations by Jewish notables or members of various elites, this was no longer the main or sole mode of activity but was auxiliary to organizational modes of representation and the public airing of issues of Jewish concern.

Toward the end of the nineteenth century in Eastern Europe, modern Jewish politics took a turn in the direction of auto-emancipation. Jews as a group now sought to determine and take responsibility for their own political fate, as evidenced by various movements for autonomism and, most notably, Zionism.[3] Over time, sympathy for these movements among Jews in Western democracies gave modern Jewish politics in these countries an international dimension. It now included seeking governmental action to ameliorate the plight and secure the rights of oppressed Jews in other countries and support for the national rights of the Jewish people. Thus, Jewish communities in various countries became involved in activities to influence their governments' conduct of foreign relations.

Modern Jewish politics was thus characterized by a formally equal Jewish citizenship status even if this was not always secured in practice; by resort to rights in order to secure, maintain, protect, or improve that status; and by the political mobilization of Jews and the public pressing of Jewish concerns by organizations and communal bodies seeking to persuade political, executive, and judicial authorities, as well as other groups and the public at large, of the validity of Jewish claims.

By and large, such politics sought to influence public policy from the outside, without getting directly involved in the formal structures that exercised power and possessed authority.[4] While in general such a stance characterizes interest groups in democracies, among Jews it was reinforced by the sense of being a vulnerable minority of social outsiders who lacked full acceptance and who either suffered or feared social rejection.

The new Jewish politics does not completely replace modern Jewish politics; rather it builds upon and enhances it. While most fully developed only in the United States, some of its features can also be found elsewhere. In brief, the new Jewish politics reflects the recent political transformation of American Jewry. Over the past two decades, both as individuals and as a group, American Jews have assumed a more active role, enhanced their status, and increased their influence within the American political system.

Previously, American Jews were politically weak and insignificant. They were hampered in the pursuit of their political interests by an inhospitable social and cultural environment that tended to make them and their leaders somewhat equivocal in asserting their claims and in giving public prominence to them. As a group, their needs were not always viewed sympathetically, and on occasion their legitimacy was questioned, if not denied outright.

Today, American Jewry is widely regarded as a significant and influential political force that exercises considerable political power. Issues of direct and immediate concern to Jews figure prominently on the American political agenda, engaging the continuous and close attention of the White House, the administration, Congress, and the media. Jewishness, per se, has become politically salient. Once political outsiders, American Jews have become political insiders.

The development of the new Jewish politics has involved a transformation in American Jews' perception and ordering of their basic ethnic concerns—consolidating and improving Jewish social, economic, and cultural status in America; enhancing relations between the United States and Israel; and ensuring Jewish survival[5]—and an even greater transformation in how these concerns are pursued.

Social, Economic, and Cultural Status

American Jews believe that to conserve and enhance their status in American society they must defend it from two major hostile pressures: the threat of anti-Semitic prejudice and discrimination, and the threat of Christianity—that is, the incorporation into American society and public life of Christian symbols, practices, and values.

Although discrimination and prejudice against Jews in America have declined, especially since the 1950s, those manifestations that continue to exist, together with the experience of Jewish history, lead many American Jews to believe that anti-Semitism is endemic in America (as in other Western societies) and affects all sections of the population, including elite groups. However benign conditions may seem, however open the institutional structures of society may be, and however great their actual participation in those structures even at the highest levels, American Jews do not feel completely secure because the *potential* always exists for things to become worse, particularly if economic and social conditions deteriorate.[6]

American Jews perceive a second threat to their group status in the direct and indirect social and cultural pressure of Christian America. Christianity is the formative cultural system for the vast majority of Americans, in terms of both values and emotions. In this sense, Jews regard American *society* as Christian, despite the formal constitutional guarantees aimed at ensuring the neutrality of the *state* with regard to religion. Consequently, for American Jews, Christianity is not merely the religion of the majority of their fellow Americans—a relatively neutral aspect of social diversity—but is rather a fundamental feature of their own status definition. Jews reject Christianity at the rational level as essentially false, and even more strongly at the affective level as the theological source of a long history of anti-Semitism and persecution. Under such conditions, they define their Jewishness, in part, in terms of its distinction from, and rejection of, Christianity. To be Jewish in America, therefore, means, among other things, to be *not* Christian.

This translates politically into a strong commitment to the separation of church and state. While many other Americans share this conviction on ideological or pragmatic grounds, its meaning to American Jews is fundamentally different. No group in America has a greater investment in separation of church and state than the Jews, for it defines their individual and group status in American society. To breach separation—to Christianize America—would relegate Jews and other non-Christian religious groups to second-class citizenship. Thus, a prime concern of Jewish politics in America is to ensure that this does not occur, supporting the maintenance of a society that is strictly neutral in matters of religious affiliation.

America may be the most tolerant, welcoming, pluralistic, and opportunity-laden society in Jewish history. Jews may be freer, more accepted, more integrated, and more successful there than in any other country in the diaspora. Yet, the threats of anti-Semitism and Christianity both continue to jeopardize Jewish equality. As a result, American Jews suffer from a permanent sense of insecurity and vulnerability only heightened by the fact that they have come so far and have so much to lose. Much of their political activity seeks to overcome such threats.

Relations with Israel

In common with many other Americans who maintain a sense of national, linguistic, and cultural identification with their homelands, American Jews care deeply about Israel and seek to enlist the support of the United States for it. At first, this concern was tinged with ambivalence. In the 1950s pride in and support for Israel were accompanied by a distinct sense of separateness and distance, and some apprehension that too close an identification might harm Jewish status in America. Eventually, however, commitment to Israel became a central element in American Jewish identification and self-definition and a focal point of its organizational and political activity. This process has gone so far that today, the future strength and vitality of American Jewish life are thought to be dependent upon Israel.[7]

American Jewish pride in Israel has focused particularly on the existence of sovereign Jewish political power, which contrasts so dramatically with the situation of Jewry during the Holocaust. Israel has also enhanced Jewish status in America by placing American Jews in the same category as other ethnic groups, which have homelands to which they relate, no longer regarded as a dispersed and rootless people. That Israel was a progressive, democratic, pioneering, egalitarian society embodying universal prophetic moral and social values, and at the same time was self-reliant and courageous and had proved that Jews could fight to defend themselves against much greater odds, added to their enhanced status in America and reinforced their positive self-image. Israel, then, is a prime focus of American Jewish self-worth and shared identity, simultaneously affirming common roots, individual personality needs, and collective aspirations. Caring for Israel, supporting it, involvement in its life and its problems are self-evident to Jews, and an extension of caring and concern for one's family.

But the dominant element in American Jews' relations with Israel has been concern about its security, which since the end of the 1960s has to a great extent become dependent upon the political, economic, and military assistance of the United States. Their primary goal, therefore, has been to ensure American support for Israel. Any indication of a weakening of that support generates anxiety and apprehension as well as intensive political activity.

The Elemental Issue of Survival

The concerns of ensuring equality for Jews and support for Israel spill over into a third concern—Jewish survival. The concern with status in America is set against a long history of anti-Semitic persecution, culminating in the Holocaust. The constant threat to Israel's security directly raises fears about the physical survival of its Jews and doubts about the future of American Jewry should Israel go under.

For about a generation after the Holocaust, its meaning as a historical event had little impact on the political behavior of American Jewry.[8] By the mid-1960s, however, it began to have an effect. In 1967, when a beleaguered Israel faced a battle for survival just prior to the Six-Day War, the lesson of the Holocaust was dramatically imprinted on the consciousness of American Jews. Established in order to provide a safe haven for Jews from the ineradicable evils of anti-Semitism, by some twist of historic irony the independent Jewish state suddenly seemed the likely scene of another Holocaust. And, once more, the Jews appeared to stand alone.

Neither the swift Israeli victory of 1967 nor the slower, more costly military success of 1973 weakened the influence of the felt analogy with the Holocaust. American Jews came to recognize that Israel's survival was permanently in question, since the loss of one war would mean the annihilation of its Jewish inhabitants. As a result, concern with survival came to pervade American Jewry's collective identity, affecting its perception of its status and role in American society and becoming the central focus of American Jewish politics.[9]

From the Liberal Politics of Individual Rights
to a Pluralist Politics of Group Survival

Modern Jewish politics in America in the 1950s and the 1960s was informed by the liberal politics of individual rights, which reflected the predominant concern of American Jews with securing equality of social, economic, and cultural status in America.

Having witnessed and been affected by the rise in anti-Semitic prejudice and educational, economic, residential, and social discrimination during the 1920s and 1930s, and spurred on by the events of World War II, the major defense organizations of American Jewry made it their main goal to seek conditions that would enable Jews fully to enter American society as equal citizens. From the mid-1940s until about the mid-1960s the central problem confronting Jews in America was defined in individual terms—the full integration of individual Jews into society, where they could enjoy their rights as citizens free of discrimination. The National Jewish Community Relations Advisory Council (NJCRAC) put it this way in 1953:

> The overall objectives of Jewish community relations are to protect and promote equal rights and opportunities and to create conditions that contribute to the vitality of Jewish living. . . . These opportunities can be realized only in a society in which all persons are secure, whatever their religion, race or origin. . . . Freedom of individual conscience is a basic tenet of American democracy. The right of each person to worship God in his own way is the keystone in one of the major arches of our national edifice of personal liberties. Government must protect this right by protecting each in the pursuit of his conscience and by otherwise remaining aloof from religious matters.[10]

Jews regarded established and advantaged groups—business, religious, academic, and social elites—as the major source of anti-Jewish prejudice. Their discriminatory activities, however, ran counter to the liberal and egalitarian values of the Constitution. In seeking to right such wrongs, therefore, Jews sought to have America live up to and practice its own highest ideals.

American Jews also manifested support for these ideals in elections and in public-opinion surveys. They preferred the Democrats—in presidential elections by margins of 18 percent to 36 percent more than the population at large, and in congressional elections by even more. Such stable Jewish partisan loyalty was closely associated with strong support for liberal political, social, economic, moral, and cultural values. Identification between liberalism and Jewishness was very high. To be sure, some Jews voted Republican, but they, too, generally supported the liberal ideals of economic and social justice. Thus, they viewed Republican candidates such as Eisenhower as liberals, and were attracted to the liberal wing of the Republican Party. What distinguished them from Jews who voted Democrat was not, therefore, opposition to liberalism, but greater social integration with non-Jews. [11]

This political pattern dominated because it provided individual Jews and the organized Jewish community in America with a coherent world view that simultaneously met particular Jewish ethnic concerns and more universal goals. It joined together the American creed, liberal ideals, Jewish values, Jewish partisan affiliations, and Jewish coalition partners in the belief that the achievement of individual liberal values and goals would necessarily satisfy Jewish concerns. In practice, Jews were allied with others in a universal struggle for a better society for all, as exemplified in Jewish support for the civil-rights movement.

The coherence of this political approach began to disintegrate at the end of the 1960s due to the impact of ethnic pluralism, whose two main features were the legitimation of claims upon American society in group terms and the rise of public and militant ethnic assertiveness. The resulting change in the focus of American Jewish politics is evident in the striking contrast between the NJCRAC 1953 statement cited above and the following statement by the same organization in 1984:

> Jewish community relations activities are directed toward enhancement of conditions conducive to secure and creative Jewish living. Such conditions can be achieved only within a societal framework committed to the principles of democratic pluralism; to freedom of religion, thought and expression; equal rights, justice and opportunity; and within a climate in which differences among groups are accepted and respected, with each free to cultivate its own distinctive values while participating fully in the general life of the society. . . . The Jewish community has always been profoundly aware that maintaining a firm line of separation between church and state is essential to religious freedom and the religious voluntarism which foster the creative and distinctive survival of diverse religious groups, such as our own.[12]

The societal legitimation of distinctive group values and diversity reinforced and heightened American Jews' already growing particularistic concerns with Israel and with Jewish survival, and the urgency of these issues tended to divert attention from their universal concerns, a process that was reinforced by growing lack of sympathy for basic Jewish ethnic concerns among some liberal groups. In addition, direct conflicts of economic interest between Jews and other ethnic groups weakened or broke up long-standing coalition arrangements; erstwhile liberal and ethnic allies now became political opponents.

To be sure, American Jews as individuals did not move far from their previous pattern of liberal political attitudes and Democratic partisan loyalties. But as a group they developed a new political approach. The liberal politics of individual rights gave way to a pluralist politics of group survival that formed the basis for the new Jewish politics.

The New Jewish Politics

Some of the main features of the new Jewish politics are well captured in the following excerpts from an address by a key official to the 1985 Annual Policy Conference of the American Israel Public Affairs Committee (AIPAC):

> 40 years ago—April 1945—we had failed. We didn't know then the extent of our failure, but we knew we had failed. And, for many of us . . . that failure has haunted us and driven us and provided us with the internal fuel needed to create a politically active people pledged to survival. . . .
>
> In our modern world, Jews have been torn between a desire for maximum integration in the general culture on the one hand and the will for Jewish survival on the other. But, the aftermath of the Holocaust, the creation of the State of Israel, and then in 1967 and 1973 the experience of almost losing what it took the murders of six million to create, drove home the urgency of putting Jewish survival first. I believe that today we recognize that if we fail to utilize our political power we may be overwhelmed by our adversaries throughout the world. We understand that if that happens, Jewish existence itself is endangered. . . .
>
> As we have bitterly learned, it is when we assume too low a profile and fail to develop economic and political power, that we are perceived as having no vital societal role. That is what makes us dispensable—that is

what made Polish Jewry dispensable in the 1930s. *NEVER AGAIN.* . . .

The specter of *dual loyalty* still haunts our community. . . . But here, in this country of ours, we ought not be shy about our interest in Israel. This is a pluralistic society and our survival here is dependent upon that pluralism. . . . Our concern for Israel does not erase our concern for America's domestic policies nor, in fact, does it mean that we do not have such concerns. . . .

We care to the depths of our souls about what happens to both the United States and Israel—that caring is not inconsistent—it is not un-American—and *it is not dual loyalty*. It is part of democracy.[13]

The Group Demand for Power

The primacy accorded group survival—focused upon, but not confined to Israel—has led directly to a group demand for political power as the only way to ensure that survival. Such a quest for power is made possible by the pluralism of American society and its democratic political system.

The group demand for power which lies at the heart of the new Jewish politics requires American Jewry as a group actively to participate in the making of public policy on matters that affect it. To exercise power in this context means to have input into the decision-making process and thereby to gain some influence over the content and direction of political outcomes. While power in this sense can be exercised without occupying public office or possessing formal authority, it cannot be attained without organization and ongoing and direct involvement in the political process.

Integrating the Jewish and American Political Agendas

A distinctive feature of the new Jewish politics and a striking indication of its interaction with the political system is the integration of the Jewish political agenda and organizational framework into the mainstream of American politics. Jewish issues have become part of the warp and woof of America's routine political agenda. Jewish concerns have become Americanized. They are adopted, promoted, shaped, and responded to by leading American political figures, including the president, cabinet members, key administration officials, and congressional leaders, and not just by Jews.

The most prominent Jewish concern embedded in American politics is Israel. Following the marked increase in the level of American foreign aid and defense assistance to Israel, particularly after the Yom Kippur War of 1973, such appropriations have become regular items on the congressional agenda. This tendency is reinforced by the country's continuing role as Israel's main source of military supplies and by its increasingly active part in Middle East peacemaking since 1967. Israel has thus become important in both congressional and presidential legislative and electoral politics, and its problems receive constant and disproportionate media coverage.

From the early 1970s until 1989, Soviet Jewry was a second significant Jewish concern demanding political and executive decisions at the highest level. Jewish political activity succeeded in making it part of the more general question of America's response to the situation of human rights in the Soviet Union and a litmus test of Soviet behavior in the larger context of American–Soviet relations. Soviet Jewry's right to emigrate and its freedom to maintain its cultural and religious life in the Soviet Union were major discussion items at summit meetings between Ronald Reagan and Mikhail Gorbachev and those between the U.S. secretary of state and the Soviet foreign minister. The issue was dramatically highlighted by symbolic gestures such as Secretary Shultz's Seder with refuseniks at the U.S. embassy in Moscow and President Reagan's meetings with prominent refuseniks such as Natan Sharansky after their release. In 1989, the Soviet Union, in no small part due to previous U.S. pressure and its desire for good relations with the United States, relaxed emigration restrictions for Soviet Jews. Because under the Reagan administration the United States had introduced a quota for the admission of Soviet refugees, in the ensuing years hundreds of thousands of Soviet Jews emigrated to Israel.

Such U.S. actions and policies were in no small measure the outcome of discussions by American Jewish leaders with the president and the secretary of state and with State Department officials, and reinforced by congressional contacts. A broad bipartisan Congressional Coalition for Soviet Jews was established in the Ninety-ninth Congress to keep members and their staffs informed on developments in the Soviet Union; there was also an active group of Congressional Wives for Soviet Jewry.

Commemorating the Holocaust has also become interwoven with the domestic American political agenda, although in a somewhat more sporadic manner. Thus we have seen the establishment of the President's Commission on the Holocaust (now called the United States Holocaust Memorial Council) and the creation of a United States Holocaust Memorial Museum in Washington. The Holocaust issue erupted into a major public debate and controversy in 1985 when President Reagan announced his intention to visit the German military cemetery at Bitburg and place a wreath there honoring the war dead of both countries. His refusal to change these plans after it became known that SS officers were buried there raised questions about America's relationship to the victims of the Holocaust, on the one hand, and their Nazi oppressors, on the other.

All of these issues illustrate the militant public self-assertiveness of American Jews that characterizes the new Jewish politics. The Soviet Jewry Mobilization Rally held on the Washington Mall on December 6, 1987, attended by some 250,000 American Jews and a large number of government officials, congressmen, and presidential candidates, was the most dramatic example in a long string of public Jewish rallies for such causes. It was distinguished only by its national scope, the extent of Jewish political mobilization, the sophistication of organizational coordination, the scale of the media coverage, and the public impact.

The integration of the Jewish and American political agendas was clearly reflected in the address to the rally of then–vice-president George Bush, who declared, with what turned out to have been considerable political foresight, that he did not want to "see five, six, ten [Soviet Jews] released at one time, but tens or hundreds of thousands of those who want to go." Although, Bush said, it would be "easier and more diplomatic to drop the human rights issue" in U.S.-Soviet negotiations, this "would be untrue to ourselves and break our promise to the past." His address also indicated that these issues were interrelated, not just for Jews but in his mind as well. In a poignant and pointed reflection on the events of the 1940s, he added: "I came away from Auschwitz determined not just to remember the Holocaust, but determined to renew our commitment to human rights around the world."

Becoming Political Professionals and Insiders

The presence of Jewish issues and concerns on the American political agenda goes only part of the way in meeting American Jews' quest for power, the pursuit of influence over the content and direction of political outcomes that matter to them. An essential contribution to that goal is made by the direct, ongoing, and increasingly professional participation of American Jews in the political process at many levels, thus increasing their input into political decisions and policy making.

Prior to the advent of the new Jewish politics, American Jews as a community were by and large political outsiders, only intermittently involved in the political process and mobilized on an ad hoc basis to meet the various crises that erupted. On such occasions, entry into the White House was generally gained via individual Jews who were major contributors and fundraisers for the political parties, often personal friends of the president, and sometimes leaders of major Jewish organizations. The overall pattern, therefore, was one of sporadic representations mainly to the White House and the administration, followed by an exit from the political arena when the issue was resolved, and concentration upon internal ethnic pursuits and community relations until the next critical issue arose.

Now, Jewish organizations and professionals involved in the pursuit of Jewish ethnic concerns are professionals and insiders in American politics. For them, the political process is a day-to-day operation, very complex, fast-moving, and fluid, subject to short-term and shifting coalitions and alliances as well as to longer-term loyalties. To keep abreast of politics under such conditions necessitates full-time, skilled, sophisticated, and professional organization, both in Washington and across the country, that is able to keep on top of complicated and sometimes obscure legislative procedures, strategems, and maneuvers. It must be capable of dealing with a whole range of complex policy questions, often demanding a high level of scientific or technological expertise, a grasp of politics that comes only with direct and intimate political experience, and the capacity to make decisions quickly in the light of these considerations. This is no game for amateurs.

The most striking illustration of the development and practice of the new Jewish politics is the American Israel Public Affairs Committee (AIPAC). Attempts to muster American support for Israel were initiated in the early 1950s by I.L. Kenen on behalf of the American Zionist Council. Although it registered with Congress as a domestic American lobby, pro-Arab and State Department circles exerted pressure on it to register as an agent of a foreign government, perhaps the ultimate symbol of outsider status. In response to this pressure, in 1954 the American Zionist Committee for Public Affairs was established as an independent and separately funded entity, which in 1959 changed its name to the American Israel Public Affairs Committee in order to strengthen its organizational base by gaining the support of non-Zionists.[14] Its goal remains today as it was formulated then: "promoting strong and consistently close relations between our country and Israel."[15]

Today, AIPAC has a nationwide grassroots membership of over 50,000, and its budget and full-time professional staff have grown dramatically. Until 1973 Kenen was the only registered lobbyist and the organization could be described as a tiny shoestring operation. By the end of the 1980s there were six lobbyists, a staff of over 100, a budget of over $10 million.[16] The committee monitors congressional activity relating to Israel, and this, too, has expanded over the years (in 1987 an AIPAC report noted that forty-seven separate Israel-related items were then at various stages of the congressional process).[17] Of particular significance in keeping abreast of these issues is close and ongoing cooperation with congressional staff members. This is in line with the established pattern in Congress whereby much legislative activity is transacted by the staff, with elected representatives often becoming involved only at the last stages, when a decision or a vote is required.[18]

The transformation of AIPAC's status in Washington is epitomized in the different career patterns of the three leading officials it has had since its inception. Its founder, I.L. Kenen, served as an official of the American Zionist movement. His successor, Morris J. Amitay, had worked for the State Department as a foreign service officer and subsequently served as a legislative aide to Senator Abraham Ribicoff. He was succeeded by the current executive director, Thomas Dine, who had been a Peace Corps volunteer and then worked in the Senate for ten years as an aide to senators Edward Kennedy, Edmund Muskie, and Frank Church. Before coming to AIPAC, Dine had no known Jewish affiliations and few even knew that he was Jewish. Similarly, many people who have served as AIPAC lobbyists had previously worked as congressional aides and have gone back to such work or established themselves as political consultants and private lobbyists after leaving AIPAC. Here, too, AIPAC is similar to the many Washington-based lobbying and consulting firms whose staff members follow the same career pattern.[19]

To supplement its Washington lobbying, AIPAC uses grassroots organization in congressional districts to mobilize "key contacts"—

AIPAC members who have direct and prompt access to congressmen and senators through political, professional, or personal connections. AIPAC members or leaders from particular regions or areas will often come to Washington during the year to lobby their representatives; these activities peak during the annual AIPAC Policy Conference, when 1,500 or more activists meet with their representatives in Congress. This pattern has recently been emulated by many other Jewish organizations, which now undertake missions to Washington on a local or regional basis or hold national meetings there. In each case the scenario is repeated: Jews from all over the country call on their congressmen and senators to make them aware of the Jewish political agenda.

The process also works the other way. A major feature of AIPAC's policy conferences are addresses by senior Cabinet members and a high turnout of legislators. For example, at the 1987 conference 307 legislators attended, including 86 Senators (48 Democrats and 38 Republicans) and 221 Representatives (134 Democrats and 87 Republicans). During presidential primary season, most candidates attend, make their views on Israel known, and contact potential campaign contributors. Such meetings are common also in major cities (particularly New York) where Jewish community relations councils host functions with leading politicians and candidates. This is, in some cases, an expression of gratitude for past support on issues of Jewish concern, but often it also serves to introduce candidates to the Jewish community. Even congressional candidates from all over the country make the rounds of such Jewish organizational events—often very distant from their constituencies—in order to make themselves and their views known to American Jewry.

The new Jewish politics is further integrated into the structures and rhythm of the American political system via an extensive network of PACs (political action committees), which maximize Jewish electoral influence. Currently, over eighty PACs seek to generate congressional support for Israel by raising funds and allocating them to candidates who have supported or are pledged to support pro-Israel policies. The largest and most significant of these is the National Political Action Committee (NATPAC), situated in Washington, which is nationally organized; most of the others are local.[20]

In all, pro-Israel PACs raised $6.2 million in the 1985–86 electoral cycle and contributed about $3.2 million to candidates for Congress.

This was approximately 2.9 percent of total giving by PACs in 1986 and less than 1 percent of the cost of electing a Congress ($450 million). But the significance of the pro-Israel PACs is greater than these proportions indicate. First, although the maximum that each PAC may contribute to a candidate is $5,000, PACs tend to concentrate on specific candidates in crucial races, particularly in the Senate, thereby magnifying the PAC impact. Thus, for example, the leading recipient of pro-Israel PAC money in 1986 received over $200,000. Second, PAC contributions to candidates are only part of the total picture. The same candidate may for the same reasons attract individual contributions and personal independent expenditure. Third, because Democrats generally are less well funded than Republicans, the traditional liberal Jewish pro-Israel contribution can be crucial. According to one analysis, it assisted the Democrats in unseating six incumbent Senate Republicans in 1986, despite the fact that the latter outspent the Democratic challengers by margins as wide a two to one. Pro-Israel PACs, then, helped shift control of the Senate from the Republicans to the Democrats.[21]

The recent proliferation of the PAC phenomenon has significantly facilitated the development of the new Jewish politics. By limiting the amount of money that individuals may contribute to electoral expenses, whether to candidates, parties, or PACS, and limiting also the amounts that PACs may contribute to candidates, the electoral laws have lessened, but not eliminated, the influence of large contributions by very wealthy individuals, which used to be a key aspect of Jewish involvement in American politics. At the same time, these laws confer a relative advantage upon those who can mobilize many small contributions, such as the existing Jewish fundraising network which specializes in soliciting contributions from many individuals. This network can thus be utilized to tap political contributions for the promotion of Jewish concerns.

PACs reinforce the new Jewish politics in three ways. First, they integrate the organized Jewish community structure into the ongoing operations and structures of the American political system by giving the group a direct say in the electoral process, as voters, contributors, and activists. Second, they directly mobilize large numbers of Jews into politics as individuals. The process may begin with a campaign contribution, but it often leads to campaign activity, lobbying, party membership, and so forth. Third, the laws that structure PAC activities make the new Jewish politics truly national. The focus on concerns that can be met only in Washington and the possibility of supporting candidates anywhere in the country based on their positions on issues give American Jews influence even in states and districts where there are few Jews. This also encourages Jewish organizations to think more on national lines and less in terms of their own organizational, local, or regional interests. One obvious manifestation is the increasing tendency of Jewish organizations and umbrella bodies to open Washington offices.

The Jewish members of Congress clearly demonstrate the integration of Jews into the structures of American politics that is central to the new Jewish politics. These individuals palpably meet the community's demand for power—the desire for control over policy outcomes on matters of ethnic concern—by direct participation in the policy-making process. They also symbolize Jewish achievement of insider status in the political system. Particularly striking has been the numerical increase of such officeholders. In 1971 there were twelve Jewish members of the House of Representatives, and two Jewish senators, but in 1991 this had increased to thirty-three Jewish House members, many from districts without any appreciable Jewish constituencies, and eight Jewish senators. Moreover, there has been a degree of partisan realignment among them. In the past, the great majority were Democrats, but recently about a quarter have been Republicans.

What is more, the Jewish members of Congress today generally have deep, strong, and public Jewish commitments that are integral to their political style and their conception of their role. A survey in the mid-1970s of the twenty-four Jewish members of the Ninety-fourth Congress found most of them actively and openly identified with the Jewish community. They publicly acknowledged and pursued Jewish interests. Not surprisingly, they were more sympathetic to Israel than their non-Jewish colleagues: in fact, their views about the Arab-Israeli conflict were well within the mainstream of opinion in the organized American Jewish community. For that reason one scholar described them as an "in-house lobby" for Israel. [22]

A more extensive and detailed survey in 1986–87 of the Jewish members of the Ninety-ninth Congress showed a similar pattern.[23] It demonstrated that almost all of them attached great importance to their Jewishness, and were highly committed to Israel. Sixty percent had a background of leadership and strong organizational involvement in the

Jewish community before their election, and five out of six belonged to a synagogue or temple both before election and currently. About nine in ten observed some Jewish rituals (Passover Seder and Hanukkah candles), and stayed home from work on the High Holidays. All contributed to the United Jewish Appeal/Federation and subscribed to a Jewish periodical. About eight out of ten said that all or most of their closest friends are Jewish.

Approximately 75 percent of these congressmen believed that being Jewish had a positive impact on their political careers, and only one perceived a negative effect. Close to a third reported that they had become more Jewish and more positive about Israel since their election: none reported a weakening of these commitments. All had visited Israel—about half of them for the first time after their election—and regarded issues specially affecting Jews as important aspects of their congressional role. About half reported that such issues sometimes created conflict in their fulfillment of their congressional role, but none felt that this conflict was constant or even usual. They tended to resolve such conflicts through informal consultations with each other and with Jewish organizational leaders.

Unlike the African-American and Hispanic members of Congress, the Jewish members do not have a formal caucus. On the one hand, this indicates the high degree of consensus among them on Jewish concerns and the effectiveness of informal consultation, which preempts the need for a formal caucus. On the other hand, it reflects the belief of Jewish congressmen that they should personally fulfill their public role in a manner that broadly integrates general and Jewish interests and confirms the balance between them, a strategy that would be disturbed by a formal Jewish caucus. As one put it, "It would be an unwanted element, unfortunately; others are expected to have a caucus, we are not." It could, another believed, "harm Jewish interests by narrowing rather than broadening congressional support of Jewish causes." According to a third legislator, there is a "fear of anti-Semitism." Overall, however, Jewish congressmen believe that there is less anti-Semitism in Congress than in the United States as a whole: just over one-third agreed that there is "little or no anti-Semitism in the United States today," but nearly three-quarters found little or none among members of Congress.

These Jewish commitments of Jewish members of Congress help maintain congressional support for Israel. By and large, since congressmen are overloaded with work, they concentrate on areas that interest them and on matters for which they are responsible. On other subjects they tend to be guided by congressmen who are considered experts, irrespective of party. Two groups that are particularly influential on matters affecting Israel are the Jewish members of Congress in general, and the members of the House Foreign Affairs Committee, in particular its Middle East subcommittee. There is significant overlap between the two groups: in 1984, 30 percent of the members of the Middle East subcommittee were Jewish, and by 1987 this had risen to 38 percent.

Congressional support for Israel is reinforced by the electoral impact of identifiable Jewish communities in over 380 congressional districts. Though Jews are only a very small proportion of the electorate, their commitment to Israel is intense and actively mobilized. What is more, public-opinion polls generally indicate greater sympathy and support for Israel than for the Arabs, and very little outright opposition to Israel. Under such conditions, members of Congress stand to benefit greatly by supporting Israel, and to gain nothing—if not lose a great deal—by opposing it.[24]

The success of the new Jewish politics in generating and maintaining congressional support for Israel must be set within a broader context of factors that encourage effective Jewish political activity. Over 80 percent of Jewish members of the Ninety-ninth Congress said that three factors—"shared moral and democratic values," "Israel as a strategic asset," and "shared foreign policy interests and objectives: Israel as an ally"—were "very important in determining U.S. support of Israel." These factors were marked higher than "considerable sympathy for Israel within the American public," "the activities of AIPAC and the Israel lobby," "the electoral significance of Jews and campaign financing," and "sympathy for Jews because of the Holocaust."[25]

Creating Community Consensus

Policies on issues of Jewish concern can be pursued most effectively if they are within the parameters of Jewish community consensus. In practice, on matters relating to Israel this means close organizational coordination between AIPAC and other major organizations, especially the Conference of Presidents of Major American Jewish Organizations. Until recently there was a general division of function between them: the Presidents' Conference represented the view of the organized Jewish community on Israel to the White House and the executive branch, whereas AIPAC worked through Congress to promote strong and close relations between Israel and the United States.

To ensure the necessary coordination, AIPAC is a member of the Presidents' Conference. Even more significantly, it has in recent years widened its own executive committee to include the top leaders of major national Jewish organizations, many of whom also sit on the Presidents' Conference, and on the executive bodies of other leading umbrella organizations such as the Council of Jewish Federations, the National Jewish Community Relations Advisory Council (NJRAC), and the National Conference for Soviet Jewry. Some are also well-known leaders, major donors, and fundraisers in large Jewish communities. This overlapping of organizational leadership, the close collaboration between AIPAC's professionals and lay officers in formulating major policy decisions, and good informal relations between them and lay leaders and professionals of the major agencies and umbrella organizations have made AIPAC representative of the community consensus and provide it widespread American Jewish support.

The system does not always work, however, and on occasion sudden changes of policy by AIPAC have caught some other major Jewish organizations (and members of Congress) unawares and left them pursuing policies that AIPAC no longer supported. This occurred in March 1986 over a proposed arms sale to Saudi Arabia.[26] Whatever the substantive justification for AIPAC's sudden change of attitude, a number of Jewish leaders and organizations felt aggrieved that they had not been consulted prior to the decision, which was made after Secretary of State Shultz promised AIPAC executive director, Tom Dine, and some of AIPAC's officers that the administration would attempt no further arms sales to Saudi Arabia that year. These problems of insufficient consultation and of policy differences were aired in October 1988 in a letter to the head of AIPAC from the three major community relations agencies, the American Jewish Committee, the American Jewish Congress, and the Anti-Defamation League.[27]

The professionalization of AIPAC, on the one hand, and its crucial role in creating and representing Jewish communal policy consensus, on the other hand, have led it in recent years to go beyond its focus upon Congress and to extend its formal and informal ties with the administration, particularly the departments of State and Defense and the National Security Council. Meetings are often initiated not by AIPAC, but by government officials: rather than American Jewry making representations to the administration, the secretary of state might meet with the AIPAC executive director in an attempt to persuade him to moderate opposition to certain administration proposals, thus increasing the chances of congressional approval. Similarly, the administration has often used the promise of significant foreign aid to Israel as a means of helping it overcome congressional opposition to various unpopular aspects of the overall foreign-aid bill.

Over the last decade or more, strategic, defense, trade, communications, and other relationships between the United States and Israel have widened and deepened. Often expressed in written agreements, they are structured in informal and formal mechanisms of consultation, cooperation, and joint activities between various departments within the administration and Israeli government ministries. The need to monitor policy proposals routinely both to maintain these relationships and to extend them led AIPAC in 1987 to establish a separate department to maintain contact with the executive branch. Its staff consisted mainly of professionals who had worked for or had close relations with the administration or the Republican Party that controlled it. The formal involvement of AIPAC in routine administration policy-making signified a further stage in the ongoing professionalization that characterizes the new Jewish politics.

Dual Loyalty, Divided Loyalties, and Single Loyalty

Another key aspect of policy coordination derives from frequent consultation with representatives of Israel, both in Washington and in Jerusalem. Such contacts ensure that, in seeking and maintaining American support for Israel and in lobbying for strong and close relations between the two countries, American Jews and their organizations—particularly the Presidents' Conference and AIPAC—know the views of the Israeli government. It is simply self-defeating for American Jews to promote policies that conflict with those of Israel.

Of course, the two communities may, and sometimes do, differ, particularly over what is feasible on the American political scene. But such differences must be worked out before action is taken. The American Jewish input in this process has been considerable, and Israel has learned a lot from the professional practitioners of the new Jewish politics about the realities of American politics. Although Israel is the dominant partner, and in the nature of the relationship has the last word, American Jewry makes an independent contribution, exerting influence upon the Israeli government at both the substantive and the tactical levels. American Jewish organizations are not, as they are sometimes perceived, simply another conduit for the Israeli government. One recent example was the question of Israel's relations with South Africa; American Jewish views had a significant impact on Israel's decision to cut back its ties with that country.

Such close, routine, and open contacts with Israeli officials point to another distinctive characteristic of the new Jewish politics: contemporary American Jewish political leaders and activists are generally less fearful of being accused of dual loyalties than were their predecessors during the 1950s.[28] This largely reflects the greater overall receptivity of the American political system to the involvement of foreign governments and their diplomatic representatives in the policy-making process. Officials of many countries, particularly allies of the United States, frequently discuss issues of shared interest with members of Congress and their staffs. Similarly, it is not unusual for American citizens—especially those with ethnic ties—to promote concerns that involve their ethnic homelands. Neither is it uncommon for American citizens to be retained as paid lobbyists on behalf of foreign governments.

Thus, issues necessitating a choice between the interests of two countries friendly to the United States may pit groups of Americans against each other, as in the administration proposal to supply AWACs to Saudi Arabia in 1981. The battle to gain congressional approval put the White House and the administration, paid lobbyists for Saudi Arabia, oil companies, other major corporations, and groups of Arab-Americans on the one side, with AIPAC and the major Jewish organizations on the other.

What is clear in the case of the AWACs and in other proposed arms sales to Arab countries is that for the practitioners of the new Jewish politics there exists a clear distinction between dual loyalties and divided loyalties. American Jews, concerned for their ethnic homeland, act to promote its interests by securing American support for it—and believe that U.S. foreign policy and defense requirements are best served by such support. Ties to Israel do not create divided loyalties that set off American Jews from America; on the contrary, they provide American Jews with an opportunity to weld these two loyalties into one. In the new Jewish politics, then, dual loyalties have been replaced by a single integrated concern for strong American–Israeli relations.

The new Jewish politics assumes an Israel that upholds democratic and moral values shared by the United States. If that assumption turns out to be mistaken, the capacity of American Jews to weld the two loyalties together will be undermined. By the same token, the possibility that American Jewish leaders and political activists might disagree with Israeli leaders about appropriate policies for Israel and about their impact in America, on the grounds that they fail to live up to those common values, is inherent in the new Jewish politics.

The Broader Agenda, Coalitions, and Issue Networks

Although Israel and other international issues capture the most prominence, the political agenda of the new Jewish politics—what we termed above the pluralist politics of group survival—is much broader. Based on the assumption that participation in the processes of democratic pluralism in the United States will enhance Jewish security, many Jewish organizations are active on a host of domestic political issues, entering into relationships of mutual support and understanding with other groups, which may later be reciprocated in support for Jewish group concerns.

These organizations actively pursue a broad political agenda in the national capital and in many state capitals and major cities as well. Prominent among them are the American Jewish Committee, the American Jewish Congress, the Anti-Defamation League, the National Jewish Community Relations Advisory Council, the Council of Jewish Federations, and the major synagogues and religious bodies, many of which maintain Washington offices in addition to their national offices, usually situated in New York.

Thus the organized Jewish community addresses many issues that are not directly related to Jewish survival. *On The Issues*, a December 1988 publication of the American Jewish Committee, describes that agency's "multi-issue agenda" based on AJC testimony to the Democratic and Republican platform committees in 1988. It includes specific policy recommendations on human rights, South Africa, separation of church and state, civil rights and civil liberties, poverty, family policy, energy, immigration and acculturation, public education, and campaign finance reform. Even more detailed positions on these matters are presented in NJCRAC's 1988–89 *Joint Program Plan*, as well as on the housing crisis, long-term care for the elderly, the minimum wage, the right to reproductive choice, broadcast deregulation, and AIDS.

Steady informal consultations among the professionals working for Jewish organizations in Washington over common concerns, ideas, and tactics keep the major organizations and leaders in touch with developments in the capital, make them aware of each other's positions, and contribute to the formation of community consensus. On particularly complex or critical issues, the list of participants may be extended to include a wider range of Washington political actors involved in or informed about these issues.

One result, then, of such pluralist group politics has been the formation of loose but extensive issue networks on major Jewish ethnic concerns, and their integration into the larger issue networks that have recently become significant features in American politics.[29] An issue network cuts across all the formal structures to bring together individuals and groups that are particularly concerned with an issue area in a loose, informal set of relationships that have no clear boundaries or are easily permeable. Involvement in such a network is an increasingly significant form of participation in the policy-making process that confers the capacity to influence policy outcomes.

Thus the pro-Israel community would include members of Congress, their staffs, some White House and administration officials, leaders and professionals in Jewish organizations, academics, journalists, policy planners who work for think tanks such as the Washington Institute for Near East Policy, lobbyists, PAC officials, party-affiliated bodies such as the National Jewish Coalition, and more. They intersect with various independent bodies such as the Brookings Institution, with those promoting pro-Arab policies, and with groups concerned with general foreign-policy and security questions, to form a Middle East issue network. Similarly, one can identify a Soviet Jewry issue network. Both it and the pro-Israel network intersect or overlap at one time or another with networks concerned with U.S.–Soviet relations; human rights; and South Africa, to name but a few issue areas.

Ideological Differentiation

Somewhat paradoxically, the emphases on pluralism and group survival in the new Jewish politics have been accompanied by, and in many ways encouraged the development of marked ideological differences within American Jewry.

When the liberal politics of individual rights was the regnant ideological approach of American Jews, it was believed that answers to the problems of the Jews as a group would be provided by solving those of all individuals. There was, then, no need to ask "Is it good for Jews?" While Jews had collective concerns, these were to be promoted in terms of what was good for all Americans, and not in separate group terms. The specific Jewish aspects of issues therefore tended to be consciously understated and kept out of the limelight.

The rise of ethnic pluralism led to the recognition that the protection of ethnic concerns was a matter for groups and, what is more, would be determined by the outcome of political competition among them. Ethnic politics is based upon the expectation of group conflict rather than the harmonious resolution of concerns in terms of individual rights and the general interest. American Jews, in common with other ethnic groups, began to pursue their concerns in a more openly particularistic manner. "Is it good for the Jews?" was now a legitimate and public question, one that became urgent and inescapable when Israel and Jewish survival became central to the Jewish political agenda.

As a result, while forging an impressive consensus on their major international ethnic concerns, American Jews have become more and more divided on other political questions. Not only has it become acceptable to ask "Is it good for the Jews?" but the range of political responses among American Jews to that question is ideologically more varied than in the past.

To be sure, the vast majority of American Jews are still to be found on the Democratic and liberal side of the political divide. Generally, about two-thirds of American Jews support Democratic presidential candidates over Republican candidates. No Republican candidate for president has ever received as high as 40 percent of the Jewish vote. Even the popular and extremely pro-Israel President Reagan received only 32 percent when running for reelection in 1984, and George Bush did not fare any better in 1988. In congressional, gubernatorial, state, and local government elections, Jewish support for the Democrats has by all accounts generally been even higher. (The New York mayoralty election in 1989 is a striking exception, but analysis of this race and its impact upon Jewish voters is beyond the scope of this chapter.)

Similarly, attitude surveys have found American Jews to be predominantly liberal on a whole range of issues, including welfare and social justice, civil rights, and civil liberties. Thus, American Jews have not abandoned liberal individualism entirely. Rather they have adapted it to incorporate pluralistic group politics, while organizationally and individually continuing to give strong support to many, if not all, of the same liberal principles. Indeed, they continue to support issues on which the liberal response is cast in terms of individual rights or liberties, such as welfare policies, social issues, and separation of church and state, but oppose those in which the liberal response is cast in terms of group rights, such as affirmative action programs that involve preferential treatment for disadvantaged ethnic groups.[30]

At the same time, however, there are now significant groups of politically active Jews who express ideological support for conservatism, and the Republican party, on Jewish grounds as well as on general grounds. Particularly prominent among them are a small but influential group of Jews, mainly academics, intellectuals, and writers who have taken a leading role in the formulation of neoconservatism. Jewish neoconservatism is the mirror image of Jewish liberalism: it seeks answers for Jewish ethnic concerns in broad general political principles that are applied to the whole spectrum of issues on the American political agenda.

Neoconservatives are generally characterized by a liberal past and a continuing allegiance to older liberal principles, which in their view have been radicalized and betrayed. Thus, neoconservatives oppose affirmative-action programs as reverse discrimination; generally took a hard line with regard to communism and the Soviet Union; advocate increased American defense expenditure; and support monetarist economic policies. In general, they have tended to sympathize with the Reagan and Bush administrations. On Jewish issues, they are particularly disturbed by anti-Semitism and anti-Israeli policies on the Left, among some Democrats (mainly blacks and other minorities), and among pro-Arab and pro–Third World groups. They anchor their concern for Israel's security and survival in a strong American defense posture. Before the dismantling of Soviet control and communism in Eastern Europe and the internal changes in the Soviet Union since 1985, they adopted hardline policies toward arms limitation agreements with the Soviet Union, which they regarded as the enemy of the free world, and of Israel in particular.

A very different conservatism characterizes many Orthodox Jews, particularly the ultra-Orthodox of New York City. Here the catalyst is different, stemming mainly from their opposition to liberalism in personal morality—abortion, homosexuality, pornography, the sexual revolution, the permissive society—as a threat to fundamental Jewish religious values. Indeed, it may also stem from a deep-seated rejection of modernity and secularism as a whole. The overwhelming electoral support in these circles for Reagan and Bush in the 1980s was more a matter of religious conservatism than of Republican partisanship; in congressional, state, and local elections, these Jews have also generally voted Democrat.

Jewish Republicanism took root institutionally in the 1980s with the formation of the National Jewish Coalition. This organization sought to channel Jewish conservatism—and Reagan's popularity—into steady and solid ideological, financial, organizational, and electoral support for the Republican Party, in the hope of making it the majority party within the Jewish community. Its leaders expected, as a result, to increase support for Jewish concerns in the Republican Party and in Republican administrations. The appointment to positions in the Bush Administration of a number of Jews connected with the National Jewish Coalition indicates its success in cementing Jewish links with the Republicans.

The current ideological differentiation within American Jewry has also led to conflicting perceptions of Jewish political interest. For example, does strict separation of church and state continue to serve Jewish interests? Although Jews generally oppose all attempts to Christianize America, the Orthodox community, in particular, which runs an extensive network of Jewish day schools, supports various forms of government aid, such as tuition tax credits, to parochial schools. Significantly, their spokesmen argue that a rigid interpretation of the establishment clause banning direct and indirect governmental financial assistance to private religious schools conflicts with the constitutional guarantee of free exercise, since it makes the provision of traditional Jewish education extremely difficult.

Ultra-Orthodox groups, motivated by traditional Jewish values, have joined like-minded Christian groups in active opposition to the liberal position on abortion, gay rights, and constitutional protection of pornography. Some have expressed support for silent prayer in public schools on the grounds that religion in general has positive effects on society. One Hasidic group has sought to use governmental property for the display of a religious symbol, the Hanukkah menorah, thereby breaking ranks with major Jewish organizations that are active in opposing such display of religious symbols. The extent of disagreement over what is the Jewish interest on such issues is illustrated by the decision of the American Jewish Congress and the American Jewish Committee to litigate against displays of menorahs on government property, and by the survey finding that the same proportion of American Jews (about 63 percent) opposed displays on government property of menorahs as well as Christmas manger scenes.[31]

Quite aside from Orthodox/non-Orthodox disagreements, conflicting perceptions of Jewish interest also figure in differences over affirmative action. Does the Jewish interest lie in support for equality of opportunity as measured by the old liberal standard of individual merit and achievement, which enabled Jews to overcome discrimination and quotas that excluded them? How should Jews react to programs that seek to end discrimination against minorities and undo the accumulated effect of past wrongs by departing from individual merit criteria and giving preference on the basis of group membership? How should Jews react to the possibility that preference for less qualified people on group grounds in the name of social justice and equality might disadvantage some Jews personally and directly? Even if individuals are disadvantaged in the short term, might not these programs be supported on grounds of a longer-term Jewish interest in a society free of all discrimination, and the benefit to Jews of resolving the social and economic problems that produce much anti-Semitism?

Most Jews respond by supporting what they consider economic and social justice through affirmative-action programs, but not quotas. Some on the political Left support more radical programs including quotas, while others on the Right adhere rigidly to the standard of individual achievement, opposing all affirmative-action initiatives. Each of these responses is framed in terms of both what is good for American society, and what is good for Jews.

New Threats, New Allies, Split Coalitions

The new Jewish politics has made relations with other groups in America more complex. When the liberal politics of individual rights prevailed, American Jews participated in broad liberal coalitions sharing common goals and aspirations with other groups on a wide range of issues; those who opposed any of their concerns were generally on the other side of the political divide on most other issues, too. But the pluralist politics of group survival has generated internally conflicted, or split, coalitions. On some issues, American Jews find themselves in partnership with groups that, on other issues, reject basic Jewish ethnic concerns. Managing split coalitions poses constant tensions and dilemmas. It is one thing to disagree with others, but partial rejection by coalition partners is an entirely different political experience. This has occurred recently in Jewish relations with African-Americans, Protestants, and Catholics.

Since the mid-1960s black–Jewish relations have deteriorated significantly. Growing black anti-Semitism has found public expression in statements by some African-American leaders. A 1982 survey of American anti-Semitism found that the mean level of anti-Semitism among blacks had risen since 1964; it had fallen among whites. In 1981 anti-Semitism was 20 percent higher among blacks than among whites.[32] Studies of Jewish opinion indicate that American Jews are keenly aware of black anti-Semitism.

Nevertheless, the vast majority of American Jews support vigorous enforcement of civil rights and anti-discrimination laws, social welfare programs to improve the situation of blacks and other minority groups, and initiatives to improve black–Jewish community relations.[33] The efforts of a number of major Jewish organizations to accomplish these objectives are made difficult by the overwhelming Jewish opposition to quotas and preferential hiring, policies supported by most blacks.[34]

Jewish–black cooperation is further set back by the widespread Jewish perception that African-Americans are not particularly sympathetic to Israel, and are much more likely than whites to think that Israel is not a reliable ally and that American Jews are more loyal to Israel than to the United States.[35] Israel's relations with South Africa also hurt its standing in the black community.

Jewish apprehensions about blacks have been reinforced by the prominence and political success of the Reverend Jesse Jackson. His own publicly quoted anti-Semitic remarks, and his refusal to denounce or disassociate himself from the outspoken anti-Semitism of Louis Farrakhan and others, have led to a widespread Jewish perception that Jackson is anti-Semitic. His denials, actions in favor of Soviet Jewry, dialogues with Jewish organizations, and the presence of a number of Jews on his campaign staff have not managed to dispel this image. In Steven M. Cohen's 1984 and 1988 surveys of American Jews, only 8 percent and 10 percent respectively stated the view that Jackson was not anti-Semitic, while 74 percent and 59 percent, respectively, said that he was. Add to this Jackson's pro-PLO views and widely publicized meetings with Yasser Arafat, and it is clear why he is perceived by Jews as a direct threat. The vast majority of American Jews are extremely uneasy about Jackson's influence within the Democratic party as the leader of a potentially broad liberal coalition of blacks, other minorities, and whites, as witnessed by the events at the 1988 Democratic Party Convention.

In seeking, nevertheless, to maintain what they can of the old alliance with African-Americans by supporting their claims to social and economic justice, American Jews act partly out of shared values but also out of the need for defense and self-protection. Black anti-Semitism threatens Jews from below. Their socioeconmic disadvantage makes blacks available for mobilization by demagogic political leaders if economic and social conditions worsen, with the Jews as targets for outbreaks of urban disorder and violence.

Alliances with some major Christian groups in America have also been impeded by the latters' approach to basic Jewish concerns. Any lack of sympathy for Israel and its survival on the part of Christians is, for many Jews, indistinguishable from anti-Semitic prejudice. Thus, relations between American Jews and American Catholics are affected by the Vatican's refusal to grant Israel diplomatic recognition. Similarly, American Jews have since 1967 been disturbed by the indifference of some leading mainline liberal Protestant bodies to threats to Israel's survival, which recall for these Jews Christian silence during the Holocaust.

A second complication in Christian–Jewish coalition-building comes from the pressure for a Christian America. Many of the Evangelicals associated with this movement strongly support Israel, seeing it as part of an overall divine plan. Yet, these same Christians are among the most determined opponents of the separation of church and state, and of a liberal, pluralist, open, and secular society—all of which most Jews espouse. Nevertheless, major Jewish organizations seek to maintain a dialogue and form stable alliances with Christians. Some Jewish agencies relate specifically to those denominations with political and social outlooks roughly comparable to their own. Others engage in the pursuit of common interests with Christians on such matters as welfare, housing, and assistance for the poor and aged, thereby avoiding areas of disagreement. Jews seek these coalitions not only to move toward policy agreement, but also in the hope that they may eventually lead Christians toward greater understanding of Jewish concerns. But until this occurs, the new Jewish politics will be characterized by many split coalitions involving only partial and temporary cooperation with other groups. Maintaining such arrangements is fraught with the constant tension of avoiding sensitive issues and handling disappointed expectations.

Conclusion: Politics Without Authority

The authority structure of American Jewry has changed little since the advent of the new Jewish politics. It is characterized by diversity and organizational autonomy. To be sure, rationalization and unity at the top levels of the Jewish community structure have increased somewhat, but lines of authority remain more implicit than explicit and exist more in informal organizational arrangements than in formal agreements or institutional structures.

At the same time, American Jewry remains united around the principle that no single body speaks on its behalf as a whole. It constitutes a community without formal authority, lacking a defined membership, clear boundaries, and contested democratic methods for choosing leaders. It has no mechanisms for reaching binding majority decisions, for setting priorities, or for penalizing dissidents.

So far, this informal and unstructured process for reaching decisions on issues has held up, largely because of the community's strong consensus on key issues such as Israel. But what will happen if disagreements emerge within American Jewry over the policies of the Israeli government? Already there is controversy over whether American Jewish organizations have a right to disagree with Israel's course, whether it is prudent to express such disagreements publicly in the United States rather than privately to Israeli leaders, and whether the answers to these questions would be any different if the Israeli government and public themselves were united rather than fundamentally divided.

The American Jewish community may not be able to settle such problems. How will dissension among American Jews over Israeli policies affect the new Jewish politics? On the one hand, a variety of American Jewish opinions about Israeli actions may signal the further Americanization of Jewish concerns, adding Israel to the list of political issues about which Jews can disagree. Indeed, such dissent may buttress claims for greater American support for the Jewish state by showing that American Jews reach their pro-Israel position through mutual discussion and persuasion, not automatic, reflex reactions. On the other hand, failure to resolve this and other questions could very well undermine the capacity for united political action to secure Israel's survival which is so central an element in the new Jewish politics.

At the moment, the threat of the loss of political effectiveness that would ensue if different Jewish groups promoted opposing policies toward Israel within Congress and the administration is a powerful incentive for the organized Jewish community in America to maintain unity on this issue. Whether it will continue to do so in the future remains to be seen, and until that issue is resolved the future path of the new Jewish politics will remain unclear.

Many other Jewish communities in democratic societies (Britain, Australia, Canada, France) have adopted some of the key elements of the new Jewish politics, such as the public, and often militant assertion of Jewish interests and concerns; and the centrality of Israel and Jewish survival among those concerns. These communities, however, remain within the broad parameters of what we termed modern Jewish politics. What makes American Jewry unique are the other elements of the new Jewish politics—the incorporation of Jewish concerns into the American political agenda; the integration of Jewish organizations and individuals into the structures and processes of the American political system; the degree of professionalization—in short, those elements that have helped to make American Jewry insiders in the American political process, and thereby to fulfill its quest for political power.

Notes

1. See the treatment of these issues in Eli Lederhendler, *The Road to Modern Jewish Politics: Political Tradition and Political Reconstruction in the Jewish Community of Tsarist Russia* (New York: Oxford University Press, 1989), pp. 11–35, 154–57.

2. I have dealt with the issue of political mobilization in Peter Y. Medding, "The Politics of Jewry as a Mobilized Diaspora," in William C. McCready, ed., *Culture, Ethnicity and Identity: Current Issues in Research* (New York: Academic Press, 1983), pp. 195–207.

3. See Jonathan Frankel, *Prophecy and Politics: Socialism, Nationalism and the Russian Jews, 1862–1917* (Cambridge: Cambridge University Press, 1981).

4. The existence of Jewish political parties contesting parliamentary elections in Poland and Romania between the wars is something of an exception to this general rule.

5. According to John Higham, such concerns are common to most ethnic groups in America. He adds a fourth—the group's internal integrity and cohesion—which we do not deal with here, although it is discussed below in a somewhat different context. See his "Introduction: The Forms of Ethnic Leadership" in John Higham, ed., *Ethnic Leadership in America* (Baltimore: Johns Hopkins University Press, 1978), p. 4.

6. Steven M. Cohen's studies for the American Jewish Committee, conducted almost annually since 1980, consistently show that between two-thirds and three-quarters of American Jews believe that "Anti-Semitism in America may, in the future, become a serious problem for American Jews."

7. I have examined this development in some detail in Peter Y. Medding, "Segmented Ethnicity and the New Jewish Politics," in *Studies in Contemporary Jewry*, 3 (1987): 26–48.

8. See Leon A. Jick, "The Holocaust: Its Use and Abuse within the American Public," *Yad Vashem Studies*, 14 (1981): 303–18, for an analysis of the development of the awareness of the Holocaust in the United States, for both Jews and non-Jews. See also Stephen J. Whitfield, "The Holocaust and the American Jewish Intellectual," *Judaism*, 28 (1979): 391–401.

9. For a more detailed analysis of the development of Holocaust consciousness and the question of Jewish survival, see Medding, "Segmented Ethnicity," pp. 26–45.

10. *Joint Program Plan, 1953*, pp. 3, 21. This is the annual statement by NJCRAC setting out the full spectrum of political and social issues confronting American Jews, with guidelines and recommendations for action. It is without a doubt the most comprehensive and authoritative statement of the political agenda of the organized Jewish community in America, as NJCRAC is the umbrella body of eleven national and 111 local Jewish community relations bodies.

11. Lawrence H. Fuchs, *The Political Behavior of American Jews* (Glencoe: The Free Press, 1956), ch. 6.

12. *Joint Program Plan, 1984/5*, pp. 3, 29.

13. Unpublished typescript made available by the speaker, Arthur Chotin, who was then a key AIPAC official.

14. See I.L. Kenen, *Israel's Defense Line: Her Friends and Foes in Washington* (Buffalo: Prometheus Books, 1981), for a personal history of AIPAC's early years by its founder and long-time executive officer.

15. AIPAC Policy Statement, *Near East Report*, 29 April 1985.

16. Mitchell Geoffrey Bard, *The Water's Edge and Beyond:Defining the Limits to Domestic Influence on United States Middle East Policy* (New Brunswick: Transaction, 1991), p. 12.

17. AIPAC *Congressional Report* to AIPAC Officers, Executive Committee, National Council, and Key Contacts (mimeo: 17 May 1987).

18. See Michael J. Malbin, *Unelected Representatives: Congressional Staff and the Future of Representative Government* (New York: Basic Books, 1980), for a critical analysis of the pivotal and burgeoning role of congressional staff.

19. Malbin, *Unelected Representatives*.

20. On PACs in general see Larry J. Sabato, *PAC Power: Inside the World of Politcal Action Committees* (New York: W.W. Norton, 1984).

21. The data in this paragraph are derived from Herbert E. Alexander, "Pro-Israel PACs: A Small Part of a Large Movement," a paper for the International Conference on the Domestic Determinants of U.S. Policy in the Middle East, Tel Aviv University, 1987, 19 pp. Alexander also indicates that the total number of such PACs is hard to determine, and could be as high as ninety.

22. Marvin C. Feuerwerger, *Congress and Israel: Foreign Aid Decision-Making in the House of Representatives, 1969–1976* (Westport, CT: Greenwood Press, 1979), p. 97.

23. This was conducted by the present author with the assistance of the Center for Modern Jewish Studies at Brandeis University. A mail questionnaire was sent to all Jewish members of the Ninety-ninth Congress in December 1986, with follow-ups in 1987. As a result of electoral defeat, retirement, and death, the total possible return was thirty-four. Of these, nineteen responded. No clear pattern could be detected among the nonrespondents as far as their known Jewish affiliations could be ascertained.

24. Feuerwerger, *Congress and Israel*, pp. 77–90.

25. Feuerwerger's survey of all members of the Ninety-forth Congress reached similar findings, emphasizing Israel's democratic character, the tradition of friendship between the two countries, shared foreign policy interests, and public awareness of the Holocaust.

26. See AIPAC *1986 Legislative Report*, pp. 13–16, for a detailed analysis of the long congressional battle; the successful whittling down by AIPAC of the size of the arms package; the continuing congressional opposition to the president's proposals even after they had been whittled down, and even after AIPAC (backed by the Presidents' Conference, NJCRAC, and ADL) decided not to fight, because "Israel would not be significantly threatened by the proposed package," a "major fight against this sale was not worth the expenditure of political capital," "and given the marginal threat of the weapons involved, an effort against the missiles alone would not be worth risking the overall favorable state of U.S.–Israel relations;" and finally the president's eventual success in overriding the congressional veto margins only after tremendous personal pressure on senators and congressman, including an attempt to get Jewish leaders to lobby senators in support of the sale.

27. *New York Times*, 12 October 1988.

28. See Ben Bradlee, Jr., "Israel's Lobby," *Boston Globe Magazine*, 29 April 1984; Wiliam J. Lanouette, "The Many Faces of the Jewish Lobby in America," *National Journal*, 1978, no. 18 (13 May): 748–59; Wolf Blitzer, "The AIPAC Formula," *Moment*, 6, no. 10 (November 1981): 22–28.

29. See Hugh Heclo, "Issue Networks and the Executive Establishment," in Anthony King, *The New American Political System* (Washington, DC: American Enterprise Institute, 1981), pp. 87–123.

30. See, for example, Steven M. Cohen, *The Dimensions of American Jewish Liberalism* (New York: American Jewish Committee, 1989), especially the tables, pp. 42–47.

31. Cohen, *Dimensions of American Jewish Liberalism*, p. 44.

32. See Gregory Martire and Ruth Clark, *Anti-Semitism in the United States* (New York: Praeger, 1982), p. 42.

33. Steven M. Cohen, *The 1984 National Survey of American Jews* (New York: American Jewish Committee, 1984).

34. Ibid.

35. See, for example, the reports on the February 1987 and April 1988 Roper Polls, prepared for the American Jewish Committee by David Singer and Renae Cohen.

Index

Abrabanel, 59
Abraham, in emergence of Jewish people, 5–6
Affirmative action programs, in United
States, 144, 146
African-Americans, relations with
American Jews, 147–148
Agudes Yisroel, 90, 94
American Israel Public Affairs Committee
(AIPAC), 127–128, 131–133,
137–139, 140
coordination with other Jewish
organizations, 137–138
grassroots organization of, 132–133
policy changes of, 138
policy conferences of, 133
role in administration policy making,
138–139
American Jewish Committee, 141–142
Amitay, Morris J., 132
Anti-Semitism
in France, 110, 116
in Germany, 112
in United States, 122, 123, 125, 147, 148
in Western and Central Europe, 106
Ashkenazic Jewry, sources of communal
authority, 67–79
Assimilationists, in Jewish politics
(1840–1939), 86, 89, 90, 98
Athaliah, opposition to rule of, 32
Austria, Jewish politics in, 87, 106, 107,
112–113
Eastern model of, 83
voting patterns in, 112–113
Zionism in, 87
Authority
in biblical Israel, 7
of medieval Jewish political institutions,
67–79
leadership elements related to, 74–77
sanctions related to, 72–74
in new Jewish politics, 149–150

Auto-emancipationists, in Jewish politics
(1840–1939), 94, 95, 98–99, 120

Ban of excommunication, in medieval
Jewish communities, 72–73, 74, 78
Bible
on administrative structure of Israelites, 8
constitutional principles in, 17–18, 35–36
covenant concept in, 8, 19–21
on emergence of Jewish people, 5–6
on king-priest-prophet triad, 7, 18, 21–36
on leadership in Israel, 6–7
on limitations of power of kings, 7–8
theocratic principles in, 18, 19
Bipolar historiography
concept of, 81–84
limitations of, 84–93
Black Americans, relations with American
Jews, 147–148
Brandeis, Louis Dembitz, 97
Bund organization, 90, 91, 97–98
number of members in, 92, 93
Bush administration, new Jewish politics
during, 129, 145

Campaigns, in elections of United States
candidate speeches to Jewish
organizations in, 133
political action committee contributions
to candidates in, 133–134
Central Europe, Jewish politics in,
105–117
emancipation affecting, 105, 106,
107–108
lack of studies on, 105–106
party affiliation in, 108
situational factors affecting, 107
Christian-Jewish relations
in France, 110, 111
in medieval politics, 68, 69
in United States, 122–123, 148–149

East European style of Jewish politics
    (1840–1939) *(continued)*
    internationalists in, 90–91
    leadership in, 84, 86–87, 101
    nationalism in, 83–84, 85–86, 92
    political and financial connections to
        Western Jews in, 87, 95–96
    sources of distinctiveness in, 107
    in triangle of political subsystems, 93–94
    Zionism in, 89, 90, 92–93, 95–97, 120
Economic issues
    in Israel, 13–14
    in medieval Jewish communities
        and leadership of wealthy elite, 75, 76
        taxation in, 70, 74, 76
    in new Jewish politics, 122–123, 125
Elazar, Daniel, 8, 9, 17
Elections
    in Eastern Europe (1840–1939), 89, 90
    in England, voting patterns of Jews in,
        111, 112
    in Germany and Austria, voting patterns
        of Jews in, 112, 113
    in Israel, 13
    in United States
        and candidate speeches to Jewish
            organizations, 133
        political action committee contributions
            in, 133–134
        political party affiliation of Jews in,
            125–126, 143–144
Emancipation of Jews
    in modern pattern of Jewish politics,
        120–121
    in Russia, 86–87
    in Western and Central Europe, 105, 106,
        107–108
        in England, 111
        in France, 109–110
        in Germany, 112
    in Western style of Jewish politics, 94, 99
England
    Jewish politics in, 99, 106, 107, 111–112
    Western model of, 82–83, 85
    Zionist movement in, 96
    taxation of medieval Jewish communities
        in, 70, 78
Ethnic groups. *see* Minority and ethnic
    groups
Europe, Jewish politics in, 67–117
    in Eastern countries (1840–1939),
        81–103. *See also* East European
        style of Jewish politics
    emancipation affecting, 105, 106,
        107–108

Europe, Jewish politics in *(continued)*
    in northern countries, authority of
        medieval political institutions in,
        67–79
    party affiliation in, 108, 109–111,
        112–113
    situational factors affecting, 107
    traditional pattern of, 119
    in Western and Central countries,
        105–117
Evidence rules, Maimonides on relaxation
    of, 49, 51–52
Excommunication, ban of, in medieval
    Jewish communities, 72–73, 74, 78
Ezra, reforms of, 28–29

Federalism, in Jewish political tradition, 9
Fines and sanctions, Talmudic doctrine on,
    46
France
    anti-Semitism in, 110, 116
    Jewish politics in, 99, 106, 107, 108,
        109–111
        Western model of, 82–83, 85
    medieval government in, 68
        and taxation of Jewish communities,
            70, 78

Galicia, Jewish politics in (1840–1939), 87,
    89
Germany
    anti-Semitism in, 112
    Jewish politics in, 106, 107, 108, 112–113
        Western model of, 82–83, 85
    Zionist movement in, 96

Ha-Levi, Judah, 55–56, 60
Hebrew language
    in East European style of Jewish politics,
        85, 86
    revival of, in Israel, 12
    in Western style of Jewish politics, 85
Henry IV, Emperor, delegation of authority
    to Jewish community, 69–70, 76
Herzl, Theodor, 97
Hiba Zion movement, 95
Historiography, bipolar
    concept of, 81–84
    limitations of, 84–93
Holocaust, 124
    commemoration of, in new Jewish
        politics, 129–130
Hungary, Jewish politics in, 88

Ibn Adret, Rabbi Solomon, 42, 58